"If you dream it you
can do it"
"Never say you cant"

FROM THE LIBRARY OF

Theresa D'Erminio
Book

Take Care of this Book

Take care of this book and make Jesus Christ your life!

JESUS CHRIST
HEALS

Theresa D'Ermino

Also by Charles Fillmore

ATOM-SMASHING POWER OF MIND

THE CHARLES FILLMORE CONCORDANCE

CHRISTIAN HEALING

DYNAMICS FOR LIVING

KEEP A TRUE LENT

METAPHYSICAL BIBLE DICTIONARY

MYSTERIES OF GENESIS

MYSTERIES OF JOHN

PROSPERITY

THE REVEALING WORD

TALKS ON TRUTH

TEACH US TO PRAY

THE TWELVE POWERS OF MAN

JESUS CHRIST HEALS

CHARLES FILLMORE

Unity Classic Library

UNITY® Books
Unity Village, Missouri

Jesus Christ Heals is a member of the
Unity Classic Library.

To receive a catalog of all Unity publications (books, cassettes,
compact discs, and magazines) or to place an order, call the
Customer Service Department: (816) 251-3580 or 1-800-
669-0282. For information, address Unity Books, Publishers,
Unity School of Christianity, 1901 NW Blue Parkway, Unity
Village, MO 64065-0001.

First edition 1939
Second edition 1940; eighteenth printing 1996

Marbled design by Mimi Schleicher © 1994
Cover design by Jill L. Ziegler

Library of Congress Catalog Card Number: 89-51144
ISBN 0-87159-197-9
Canada GST R132529033

Unity Books feels a sacred trust to be a healing presence in
the world. By printing with biodegradable soybean ink on
recycled paper, we believe we are doing our part to be wise
stewards of our Earth's resources.

"Any declaration man may make in which the name *Jesus Christ* is used reverently will contact the spiritual ether in which the Christ I AM lives and will open the mind and body to the inflow of spiritual healing rays."

Charles Fillmore

FOREWORD

→»-»» «-«-«««

Much has been written and said about the healing
methods that Jesus used in His very striking cures of
physical ills. The generally accepted theory is that
they were miracles, but to this there have been many
objections, among them Jesus' promise "He that believeth on me, the works that I do shall he do also."
So many millions have claimed that they believed on
Jesus, yet not only have they failed to heal others but
they have gloried in sickness and finally death under
the assumption that it was the will of God.

Few have dared even to suggest that Jesus applied universal law in His restorative methods; for
on the one hand it would annul the miracle theory
and on the other it would be sacrilegious to inquire
into the miracles of God. So it has been generally
accepted that Jesus' great works were miracles and
that the power to do miracles was delegated to His
immediate followers only. But in recent years a con-
siderable number of Jesus' followers have had the
temerity to inquire into His healing methods, and
they have found that they were based on universal
mental and spiritual laws that anyone can utilize who
will comply with the conditions involved in these
laws. This inquiry has led to the conclusion that man
and the universe are founded on mind and that all

changes for good or ill are changes of mind.

Ages of thought upon the reality and solidarity of things have evolved a mental atmosphere that has produced the present material universe. These and millions of other concepts are the work of men and not God, as is popularly supposed. However they all rest on the original God-Mind and can be restored to the perfect law and order of that Mind by those who free themselves from their mental entanglements with materiality and identify their thinking with that of the Mind that is Spirit. "Ye shall know the truth, and the truth shall make you free."

It is taught in the Bible that Jesus was born into the human family to save its people from extinction; that, according to Paul, as in Adam all died so in Christ shall all be made alive. A psychological study of the whole situation proves this to be virtually true. Millions have accepted Christianity on faith and have found peace of mind and spiritual satisfaction without understanding the fundamental mind principles on which the redemptive system rests. This is proof that there is more to Christianity than the surface acceptation of Jesus as mediator between God and man.

We are all in mind related to a great creative Spirit that infuses its very life into our minds and bodies when we turn our attention to it. We have mentally wandered away from this creative Spirit or Father-Mind and lost contact with its life-giving currents. Jesus made connection for us, and through Him we again begin to draw vitality from the great fountainhead.

Ability to pick up the life current and through it perpetually to vitalize the body is based on the right relation of ideas, thoughts, and words. These mental impulses start currents of energy that form and also stimulate molecules and cells already formed, producing life, strength, and animation where inertia and impotence was the dominant appearance. This was and is the healing method of Jesus.

Although the Bible repeatedly refers to the creative power of the Word, men have not dared to think that the creative law is universal and could be taught to any man who would discipline his thoughts and words and center them on God-Mind. Jesus gave His whole attention to God, so much so that He claimed He did not even originate the words that He spoke: they came from the Father. By careful thinking and wholehearted concentration on God, Jesus made such complete union with creative Mind that His body was transformed in the presence of His disciples. He taught that men would eventually reap the reward of every word they uttered. "For by thy words thou shalt be justified, and by thy words thou shalt be condemned."

Perfect health is natural, and the work of the spiritual healer is to restore this perfect health, which is innate and can be spoken into expression. Our ills are the result of our sins or failure to adjust our minds to Divine Mind. "Man hath authority on earth to forgive sins." When the sinning state of mind is forgiven and the right state of mind established, man is restored to his primal and natural wholeness. This is wholly a mental process, and so all conditions of man are the result of his thinking. "As he [man] thinketh in his heart, so *is* he."

No book, not even the Bible, covers all phases of human thought. Therefore the mental panacea for every ill is beyond the description of words, but Jesus Christ epitomized in His own consciousness all the thought processes necessary to man's complete restoration. So it is taught that Jesus Christ is the Word or Divine Logos in which is contained all the original creative essence.

The truth that divine man is manifest God is the great mystery hid for ages and generations and now revealed in Jesus Christ.

CONTENTS

CHAPTER I

Be Thou Made Whole

->>>->>>-<<<-<<<-

J ESUS SAW in Himself the perfect pattern of the God-Mind. He lived so close to that pattern that He became its perfect expression. As He continued to live closer and ever closer to God He beheld all men as living inventions of God, and through His spiritualized mentality awakened the image of the perfect pattern of the God-Mind in those who came to Him for help. Thus by arousing their souls' energy to such an extent that the physical became immersed in the healing life He enabled the perfect man to come into manifestation.

For example, when Jesus said in a loud voice to the spiritual man in the sleeping Lazarus who had been in the tomb four days, "Lazarus, come forth," the power of the Word in His voice aroused the spiritual man in Lazarus, who in turn awakened his soul to activity. Then the soul life in Lazarus resurrected and restored the seeming dead body, and Lazarus arose and walked out of the tomb.

The more enlightened man becomes the greater is his desire for perfect health. This is logical, for to be healthy is natural. It is a state of being sound or whole in mind, body, and soul. To heal then is to bring forth the perfect Christ man that exists within each of us.

There is quite a bit of misunderstanding on the

part of both Christians and non-Christians with regard to the meaning of the words Christ and Jesus, and their use as applied to Jesus of Nazareth. Christ, meaning "messiah" or "anointed," designates one who had received a spiritual quickening from God, while Jesus is the name of the personality. To the metaphysical Christian—that is, to him who studies the spiritual man—Christ is the name of the supermind and Jesus is the name of the personal consciousness. The spiritual man is God's Son; the personal man is man's son. In the unregenerate God's Son is a mere potentiality. But in those who have begun the regenerative process Jesus, the Son of man, is in a state of becoming the Son of God; that is, man is being born again. At the time Jesus told Nicodemus, "Except one be born anew, he cannot see the kingdom of God," He Himself was undergoing that mysterious unfoldment of the soul called the "new birth." He promised great power to those who followed Him in soul development. "Ye who have followed me, in the regeneration . . . shall sit upon twelve thrones."

The Christ or Son-of-God evolution of man's soul is plainly taught in the New Testament as the supreme attainment of every man. "For the earnest expectation of the creation waiteth for the revealing of the sons of God."

Without some evidence in us of the Christ man we are little better than animals. When through faith in the reality of things spiritual we begin soul evolution there is great rejoicing; "we rejoice in hope of the glory of God."

Christ existed long before Jesus. It was the Christ Mind in Jesus that exclaimed, "And now, Father, glorify thou me with thine own self with the glory which I had with thee before the world was."

We should clearly understand that the Christ, the spiritual man, spoke often through Jesus, the natural man; and then again the natural man, Jesus, spoke on His own account. Spiritual understanding reveals to us when it was that Christ spoke and when it was that Jesus spoke. We know that Christ, the spiritual man, could not have experienced death, burial, and resurrection. The experiences were possible only to the mortal man, who was passing from the natural to the spiritual plane of consciousness. The Christ was present with Jesus, quickening and healing His body and finally raising it to the ethereal realm, where He exists to this day.

As Christ the Son of God became manifest in Jesus so He becomes manifest in us when we follow Him in the regeneration. "The Spirit of him that raised up Jesus from the dead . . . shall give life also to your mortal bodies."

But we must have faith in Spirit and through our thinking build it into our consciousness; then our bodies will be restored to harmony, health, and eternal life.

Jesus still lives in the spiritual ethers of this world and is in constant contact with those who raise their thoughts to Him in prayer. The promise was not an idle one that He would be with those who have faith in Him. "Let not your heart be troubled, neither let it be fearful. Ye heard how I said to you, I go away, and I come unto you."

His body disappeared from our fleshly eyes because He raised it to its true place in the ether; but He can make His presence felt to anyone who looks to Him for help. "For where two or three are gathered together in my name, there am I in the midst of them."

If but two persons agree in their prayers and thoughts about Jesus Christ and His power to help, by sympathetic soul unity He instantly responds. "Again I say unto you, that if two of you shall agree on earth as touching anything that they shall ask, it shall be done for them of my Father who is in heaven."

Jesus did not go to a faraway heaven, there to abide to the great day of His "Second Coming." He explained again and again, in language that anyone who has even a slight understanding of the interrelation of spirit, soul, and body may comprehend, that He would continue to exist in the etheric realm that He called "the heavens." He appeared after His crucifixion to five hundred at one time, and to many others: notably Paul, whom He converted by talking to him out of the ether. This all confirms His promise "Lo, I am with you always, even unto the end of the world."

Paul says that we are all dead or asleep in trespasses and sins and that Jesus was the "firstfruits of them that are asleep." Physiology teaches that the body is alive to the degree that the cells are alive;

that we are carrying around many dead cells. Jesus knew how to quicken with new life the cells of His organism, and He promised that all who follow Him will do likewise.

So both Scripture and science agree that there must be a resurrection of the body from the dead; that is, the dead substance that our minds have organized into cells, tissues, flesh, and blood. The all-important task for everyone is how to get the mastery of the negative life or microbe that is reducing our bodies to corruption and final dissolution.

Paul says, "This corruptible must put on incorruption, and this mortal must put on immortality." Here is a concise statement of where resurrection is to take place. Other writings of Paul's have seemingly prophesied a great day on which all the dead are to come forth from their graves, but this would involve situations complex and contradictory beyond reconciliation. That we have all lived hundreds, even thousands, of times and have left our bodies in many lands is being accepted by logical persons everywhere. If our old bodies are to be resurrected, which of these discarded ones shall we repossess? Chemistry says that our flesh becomes again the dust of the ground:

"Imperious Caesar, dead and turned to clay,
Might stop a hole to keep the wind away."

Jesus spent whole nights in prayer according to the Gospels, and it is quite evident that He was resurrecting His body by realizing, as we do in our prayers, that God was His indwelling life. His affirmation for more life was "I am the resurrection, and the life."

I AM is the spiritual name of Jehovah, the everliving one. When we affirm, "I am," with our thoughts centered on Spirit, we quicken the life flow in the body and awaken the sleepy cells. Such affirmations clear up congested areas of the organism and restore the circulation to its normal state, health.

A prominent scientist recently stated that man's body is composed of trillions of cells, every one an electric battery. A battery emits electrical impulses of various kinds, transformable into light, power, heat. The human body is undoubtedly the most powerful dynamo in existence for the carrying on of life. The presiding ego or I AM in each organism determines the particular kind of impulse that the cells shall radiate. The field of dynamic energy is limitless. God is Spirit, and Spirit is the very essence of the ether in which we live, move, and have our being.

Affirmations of health by Christian healers right in the face of sickness often result in marvelous restorations that are sometimes called miracles of healing. But when one understands the power of words spoken in spiritual consciousness the results are in fulfillment of divine law. Jesus stated the essence of this law when He said, "Whosoever . . . shall not doubt in his heart, but shall believe that what he saith cometh to pass; he shall have it."

Every word has within it the power to make manifest whatever man decrees, but especially spiritual words have this power. God creates by the power of the word. "God said, Let there be light: and there was light." Every act of creation was preceded by

"God said." Man, the apex of God's creation, was created in His image and likeness; that is, exactly like Him in the power of his word to bring forth what he says.

In order to create as God creates man must have undoubting faith in God-Mind and the obedience of the creative electrons hidden in the atoms of all substance. In Hebrews it is written, "By faith we undertsand that the worlds have been framed by the word of God." In the 1st chapter of John the Word or Logos is given as the source of all things, and this Word is said to become flesh and be glorified as the only-begotten from the Father. "As many as received him, to them gave he the right to become children of God, *even* to them that believe on his name." Jesus said that every man would be justified or condemned by his word. He demonstrated the power of the word of faith in His mastery of natural laws and in His many marvelous healings.

Although we all get definite results in body and affairs from the words we utter, those results would be infinitely greater if we understood the power of words and had undoubting faith in their creative power. Jesus said, "The words that I have spoken unto you are spirit, and are life."

We all want to be like Jesus, and millions have made and are making Him the pattern for their life. So among His faithful followers of the past twenty centuries we should expect to find a world of glorified men and women. Why have we not brought forth more of the fruits of Spirit that He so generously promised? The answer is that we have emphasized the negative qualities as portrayed by the human side of His character. We have sought to imitate Him in our acts instead of our thoughts and words.

We are now realizing that as a man "thinketh within himself, so is he." The outer acts are secondary; the primal world of causes is within, and it is to this inner realm that we must look for the transforming power of man and of the world about him as well. "Be ye transformed by the renewing of your mind." Hence the quick and lawful way to attain health is to put your creative words to work and bring into swift action the superman Christ.

There can be no logical doubt that an all-wise and all-powerful Creator would plan perfection for His creations and also endow them with the ability to bring His plan into manifestation. That is the status of the world and its people. We are God's ideal conception of His perfect man, and He has given us the power of thought and word through which to make that ideal manifest.

It is written in John 5:21 (King James Version): "For as the Father raiseth up the dead, and quickeneth *them;* even so the Son quickeneth whom he will."

The American Standard Version says that the Father raises up the dead and gives them life, and that even so the Son gives life to whom He will. To quicken means to vivify, vitalize, energize, hence to make alive.

Jesus made this assertion of the life-giving power of the Son of God immediately after He had healed a man at the Pool of Bethesda who had been infirm and helpless for thirty-eight years. Jesus said to him, "Behold, thou art made whole: sin no more, lest a worse thing befall thee."

Here Jesus again emphasizes sin as the cause of infirmity. All the ills of humanity are the effect of broken law, of sin. That word "sin" covers more ground than we have usually granted it. There are sins of omission and commission. If we fail to cultivate the consciousness of the indwelling spiritual life, we commit a sin of omission that eventually devitalizes the organism. To be continuously healthy we must draw on the one and only source of life, God. God is Spirit, and Spirit pours its quickening life into mind and body when we turn our attention to it and make ourself receptive by trusting Spirit to restore us to harmony and health.

As for all the marvelous works that Jesus did, He never claimed His personality as their author. "The Son can do nothing of himself, but what he seeth the Father doing: for what things soever he doeth, these the Son also doeth in like manner." We all have access to the Son of God (the Christ) implanted in us by the Father-Mind if we will give it a chance to quicken us with creative ideas.

Let us remember that in declaring Jesus to be present with us we are placing ourselves in a thought atmosphere that will help us to quicken our own supermind or Christ Mind. Jesus raised His mind and body to His supermind level, permitting a life radiation without crosscurrents or discords of any kind.

He preceded us, and as He said, He had prepared a "place" for us. This "place" is a spiritual current in the cosmic ether, in which we live, and we can feel it when we direct our attention to Christ in prayer and meditation. "The kingdom of God is come nigh unto you."

Jesus called attention to the fact that the creative Mind, which He lovingly called Father, had provided for the subsistence of the birds and flowers, and that man was of more value than these; and would it not be reasonable, He argued, that the Father would also provide for man? His logic is unanswerable, and we must all admit that judging from our human ideas about providing for our children, we should expect God to have done even better for His progeny.

When we understand the nature of the creative Mind—that it is Spirit-mind, that all things come out of ideas, and that there are unlimited ideas right at the door of the mind—it dawns on us that God has provided for us beyond our fondest dreams.

We have been so persistently taught that nature heals that we do not as a rule give the question of the origin of her healing power any serious thought. But we should, because our thought calls into action in our consciousness the mind principle to which we give our attention. If we center our attention on nature as the healing principle, we stir up natural activities that are secondary to the one cause of all action, that is, infinite Mind. But it is our privilege as creations of supreme Mind to bring into action all its forces, primary and secondary. By our thought and the mighty mind energy back of thought we can stir to action all the powers of Being and get the results of their concentrated healing currents instead of the weakened, segregated seepage from one.

Just here is a good opportunity to urge Truth students to shape their spiritual unfoldment on one system of development instead of chasing after every spectacular scheme that pops up. All signs both spiritual and secular point to Jesus Christ as the appointed head of our race. Through Him we have received a philosophy of life that has been tested in the past, that is now being tested as never before, and that is proving to have no peer as a revealer of Truth and as a remedy for all the ills of humanity.

This being obvious and so many of us having received special revelations confirming it, why should we feel the lack of another or listen to the many "Lo, there! Lo, here!" proclamations of those who discern superficial things only? Concentrate your I AM attention on God as the one and only supreme Spirit and Jesus Christ as the Son of God through whom we all have access to the Father. Then you will lift your consciousness into a sphere of spiritual clarity and power superior to anything in the heavens above or the earth beneath.

Certain persons called "masters" have forged ahead of the race in their understanding and use of some of the powers of mind and have in personal egotism set up little kingdoms and put themselves on thrones.

These so-called "masters" and members of occult

brotherhoods are attracting susceptible minds away from the "straight and narrow path" and leading them to believe that there is a short cut into the kingdom. Jesus described the situation forcibly and clearly in Matthew 24:24:

"For there shall arise false Christs, and false prophets, and shall show great signs and wonders; so as to lead astray, if possible, even the elect."

Read the whole 24th chapter of Matthew. In it Jesus describes in symbols and facts what is taking place today in all parts of the world. It may be argued that these conditions have been present in every generation, and so they have; but never have so many of the signs stood out so forcibly as now. All this indicates the end of a world dispensation, a climax in race development. The end of the world of matter came with the discovery that the atom is electrical, and all the things that revolved about that material supposition are coming to an end with it. This means the end of our old ideas that God is a big man sitting on a throne in a heaven with streets of shining gold, with Jesus at His right hand writing in the book of life, as well as the end also of our ideas of Satan and his fiery hell, of the divine right of kings and the prestige of royalty and other established institutions. These crude ideas about God and man having lost the sustaining thoughts of the race, old religions and governments dissolve and the world seems a chaos. However the wise see in all this the passing away of old ideas and old things to make room for the new. "Behold, I make all things new."

The only safety from chaos is unity with God and His Son Jesus Christ, the head of every man. If we are not anchored to this supreme and immovable reality, we shall be exposed to the storms of mortal thought and shipwrecked on the rocks of materiality. "Have this mind in you, which was also in Christ Jesus."

Jesus taught that His mission was to establish the kingdom of heaven on earth. The first step in His great work was the awakening of men to certain fundamental truths of being. He taught the power of mind, thoughts, words. He cast out the demons (errors) and healed the sick with a word. He planted the seed thoughts in our race mind that will, when properly used, grow into the kingdom of the heavens here on earth. But peace, harmony, and love must first be planted in the minds of men.

Jesus gave us the consciousness of peace. "My peace I give unto you." The mind of peace precedes bodily healing. Cast out enmity and anger and affirm the peace of Jesus Christ, and your healing will be swift and sure.

CHAPTER II

God Presence

→))→))‹((‹((←

I AM NOW *in the presence of pure Being and immersed in the Holy Spirit of life, love, and wisdom.*

I acknowledge Thy presence and power, O blessed Spirit. In Thy divine wisdom now erase my mortal limitations, and from Thy pure substance of love bring into manifestation my world, according to Thy perfect law.

Man knows intuitively that he is God's supreme creation and that dominion and power are his, though he does not understand fully. The I AM of him ever recognizes the one divine source from which he sprang, and he turns to it endeavoring to fathom its wonderful secrets. Even children grope after the truths of Being.

No man knows the beginning of the query, Who, what, and where is God? It is dropped from the lips of the little child when he first begins to lisp the name of father and of mother, and it is repeated throughout the years.

Who made you? Who made me? Who made the earth, the moon, and the sun? God.

Then who made God?

Thus back to the cause beyond the cause ever runs the questioning mind of man. He would understand the omnipresence that caused him to be.

Does an answer ever come to these questionings? Does man ever receive satisfactory returns from this mental delving in the unfathomable? Each man and each woman must answer individually; for only the mind of God can know God. If you have found God in your own mind you have found the source of health, of freedom, and of the wisdom that answers all questions.

Language is the limitation of mind; therefore do not expect the unlimited to leap forth into full expression through the limited.

Words never express that which God is. To the inner ear of the mind awakened to its depths words may carry the impulses of divine energy and health that make it conscious of what God is, but in their formulations such words can never bind the un-bindable.

So let us remember that by describing God with words in our human way we are but stating in the lisping syllables of the child that which in its maturity the mind still only faintly grasps. Yet man may know God and become the vehicle and expression of God, the unlimited fount of life, health, light, and love.

God is the health of His people.

Man recognizes that health is fundamental in Being and that health is his own divine birthright. It is the orderly state of existence, but man must learn to use the knowledge of this truth to sustain the consciousness of health.

Health is from the Anglo-Saxon word meaning

"whole," "hale," "well." The one who uses the
word really implies that he has an understanding of
the law of the perfect harmony of Being. Health is
the normal condition of man and of all creation. We
find that there is an omnipresent principle of health
pervading all living things. Health, real health, is
from within and does not have to be manufactured
in the without. Health is the very essence of Being.
It is as universal and enduring as God.

Being is the consciousness of the one Presence
and the one Power, of the one intelligence, and man
stands in the Godhead as *I will*. When man perceives
his place in the great scheme of creation and recognizes his I AM power, he declares, "I discern that
I will be that which I will to be."

Man is the vessel of God and expresses God. But
there is a mighty difference between the inanimate
marble, chiseled by the sculptor into a prancing
steed, and the living, breathing horse consciously
willing to be guided by the master's rein.

So there is a wide gap between the intelligence
that moves to an appointed end under the impulse
of divine energy and that which knows the thoughts
and desires of Divine Mind and co-operates with it
in bringing about the ends of a perfect and healthy
creation.

"No longer do I call you servants; for the servant
knoweth not what his Lord doeth; but I have called
you friends; for all things that I have heard from my
Father I have made known unto you."

It must be true that there is in man a capacity

for knowing God consciously and communing with Him. This alone insures health and joy and satisfaction. It is unthinkable that the Creator could cause anything to be that is so inferior to Himself as to remove it beyond the pale of fellowship with Him.

It is our exalted ideas of God and our little ideas of ourselves that built the mental wall that separates us from Him. We have been taught that God is a mighty monarch with certain domineering characteristics, who wills us to be sick or healthy; that He is of such majesty that man cannot conceive of Him.

Even in metaphysical concepts of God the impression left us is of a Creator great in power, wisdom, and love. In one sense this is true, but the standard by which man compares and judges these qualities in his mind determines his concept of God.

If I say that God is the almighty power of the universe and have in mind power as we see it expressed in physical energy and force, I have not set up the right standard of comparison. It is true that all power comes from God, but it does not follow that the character of the thing we term power is the same in the unexpressed as in the expressed.

God is power; man is powerful. God is that indescribable reservoir of stored-up energy that manifests no potency whatever until set in motion through the consciousness of man yet possesses an inexhaustible capacity that is beyond words to express. When that power is manifested by man it becomes conditioned. It is described as powerful, more powerful, most powerful, and it has its various degrees of expansion, pressure, velocity, force, and the like.

This power is used by men to oppress one another, and there has come to be a belief that God is power in the sense of great oppressing capacity. It is an ancient belief that He can and does exercise His power in punishing His creations, pouring out upon them His vengeance.

But this is not the character of divine power. If by power we mean force, energy, action, oppression, then we should say that God has no power, that God is powerless; because His power is not like the so-called power that is represented by these human activities.

God is wisdom—intelligence—but if we mean by this that God is "intelligent," that His knowledge consists of the judgments and inferences that are made in a universe of things, then we should say that God is nonintelligent.

God is substance; but if we mean by this that God is matter, a thing of time, space, condition, we should say that God is substanceless.

God is love; but if we mean by this that God is the love that loves a particular child better than all children, or that loves some particular father or mother better than all fathers and mothers, or that loves one person better than some other person, or that has a chosen people whom He loves better than some other people who are not chosen, then we should say that God is unloving.

God does not exercise power. God is that all-present and all-quiet powerlessness from which man "generates" that which he calls power.

God does not manifest intelligence. God is that unobtrusive knowing in everyone which, when acknowledged, flashes forth into intelligence.

God is not matter nor confined in any way to the idea of substance termed matter. God is that intangible essence which man has "formed" and called matter. Thus matter is a limitation of the divine substance whose vital and inherent character is above all else limitless.

God is not loving. God is love, the great heart of the universe and of man, from which is drawn forth all feeling, sympathy, emotion, and all that goes to make up the joys of existence.

Yet God does not love anybody or anything. God is the love in everybody and everything. God is love; man becomes loving by permitting that which God is to find expression in word and act.

The point to be clearly established is that God exercises none of His attributes except through the inner consciousness of the universe and man.

God is the "still small voice" in every soul that heals and blesses and uplifts, and it is only through the soul that He is made manifest as perfect wholeness.

Drop from your mind the idea that God is a being of majesty and power in the sense that you now interpret majesty and power.

Drop from your mind the belief that God is in any way separated from you or that He can be manifested to you in any way except through your own consciousness.

We look at the universe with its myriad forms and stupendous evidences of wisdom and power and we say: All this must be the work of one mighty in strength and understanding; I should stand in awe of such a one and realize my own insignificance in His presence. Yet when we behold the towering oak with its wide-spreading branches, we say it grew from a tiny acorn. A little stream of life and intelligence flowed into that small seed and gradually formed the giant tree. It was not created in the sense that it was made full-orbed by a single fiat of will, but it grew from the tiny slip into the towering tree through the inherent potentialities of the little seed, the acorn.

So God is in us the little seed through which is brought forth the strong, healthy Christ man.

That "still small voice" at the center of our being does not command what we shall be or what we shall do or not do. It is so gentle and still in its work that in the hurly-burly of life we overlook it entirely. We look out, and beholding the largeness of the world of things, we begin to cast about for a god corresponding in character with this world.

But we do not find such a god on the outside. We must drop the complex and find the simplicity of "the most simple One" before we can know God. We must become as a little child.

Jesus said, "God is Spirit," not "a Spirit," as in the King James Version. According to Webster, the word *spirit* means life or living substance considered independently of corporeal existence; an intelligence conceived of apart from any physical organization or embodiment; vital essence, force, or energy as distinct from matter; the intelligent, immaterial, and immortal part of man; the spirit, in distinction from the body in which it resides.

Paul says, "In him we live, and move, and have our being." If we accept Scripture as our source of information there can be no higher authority than that of Jesus and Paul. They say that God is Spirit.

Spirit is not matter, and Spirit is not person. In order to perceive the essence of Being we must drop from mind the idea that God is circumscribed in any way or has any of the limitations usually ascribed to persons, things, or anything having form or shape. "Thou shalt not make unto thee a graven image, nor any likeness *of any thing* that is in heaven above, or that is in the earth beneath."

God is life. Life is a principle that is made manifest in the living. Life cannot be analyzed by the senses. It is beyond their grasp, hence it must be cognized by Spirit.

God is substance; but this does not mean matter, because matter is formed while God is the formless. This substance which God is lies back of all matter and all forms. It is that which is the basis of all form yet enters not into any form as finality. It cannot be seen, tasted, or touched. Yet it is the only "substantial" substance in the universe.

God is love: that from which all loving springs.

God is Truth: the eternal verity of the universe and man.

God is mind. Here we touch the connecting link between God and man. The essential being of God as principle cannot be comprehended by any of the senses or faculties, but the mind of man is limitless, and through it he may come in touch with divine Principle.

It is the study of mind that reveals God. God may be inferentially known by studying the creations that spring from Him, but to speak to God face to face and mouth to mouth, to know Him as a child knows his father, man must come consciously into the place in mind that is common to both man and God.

Men have sought to find God by studying nature, but they have always fallen short. This seeking to know God by analyzing things made is especially noticeable in this age. Materialistic science has sought to know the cause of things by dissecting them. By this mode they have come to say: We must admit that there is a cause, but we have not found it; so we assume that God is unknowable.

To know God as health one must take up the study of the healthy mind and make it and not physical appearance the basis of every calculation. To study mind and its ideas as health is a departure so unusual that the world, both religious and secular, looks upon it as somehow impracticable. The man who lives in his senses cannot comprehend how anything can be got out of the study of something apparently so intangible.

The man of affairs cannot see what mind or its study has to do with matters pertaining to his department of life, and the religionist who worships God in forms and ceremonies makes no connection between the study of mind and finding out the real nature of God.

Behold, I go forward, but he is not *there;*
And backward, but I cannot perceive him;
On the left hand, when he doth work, but I cannot behold
        him;
He hideth himself on the right hand, that I cannot see him.

Thus ever cries the man who looks for God in the external; for health from an outside source.

In mathematics the unit enters into every problem; and in existence mind is common to all, above and below, within and without. The secret of existence will never be disclosed before man takes up and masters the science of his own mind.

Man's consciousness is formed of mind and its ideas, and these determine whether he is healthy or sick. Thus to know the mysteries of his own being he must study mind and its laws.

Many people in every age have come into partial consciousness of God in their souls and have communed with Him in that inner sanctuary until their faces shone with heavenly light; yet the mysteries of creative law were not revealed to them, because they did not get an understanding of its key, which is mind.

Mind is the common meeting ground of God and

man, and only through its study and the observation
of all the conditions and factors that enter into its
operation can we come into the realization of God as
abiding health and sustenance.

God is mind; and we cannot describe God with
human language, so we cannot describe mind. To
describe is to limit, to circumscribe. To describe mind
is to limit it to the meanings of sense. In our talk
about mind we are thus forced to leave the plane
of things formed and enter the realm of pure knowing.

We can only say: I am mind; I know. God is
mind; He knows. Thus knowing is the language I
use in my intercourse with God.

If you ask me about the language I use in com-
municating with God, I am not able to tell you; because you are talking from the standpoint of using
words to convey ideas, while in the language of God
ideas in their original purity are the vehicles of
communication.

But ideas are the original and natural agents of
communication; and everyone is in possession of
this easy way of speaking to God and man. Thus we
may learn to use this divine and only true way consciously if we will but recognize it and use it on the
plane of mind.

But we must recognize it. This is the one truth
that we have to reveal to you: How to recognize this
divine language in your own consciousness and how
through recognition to bring it forth into visibility.
It is a truth however that we cannot reveal to you

by a series of eloquent essays on the majesty, power, and wisdom of God and on the everlasting joy that follows when you have found Him; but only by showing you in the simplest way how to come into conscious relations with the source of omnipresent wisdom, life, and love, by taking with you in the silent inner realms the first steps in the language of the soul.

Compared with audible language, communion in mind can be said to be without sound. It is the "still small voice," the voice that is not a voice, the voice using words that are not words. Yet its language is more definite and certain than that of words and sounds, because it has none of their limitations. Words and sounds are attempts to convey a description of emotions and feelings, while by the language of mind emotions and feelings are conveyed direct. But again you must transcend what you understand as emotion and feeling in order to interpret the language of God. This is not hard. It is your natural language, and you need only return to your pristine state of purity to achieve it entirely.

You are mind. Your consciousness is formed of thoughts. Thoughts form barriers about the thinker, and when contended for as true they are impregnable to other thoughts. So you are compassed about with thought barriers, the result of your heredity, your education, and your own thinking. Likewise your degree of health is determined by your thoughts, past and present.

These thoughts may be true or false, depending

on your understanding and use of divine law. You must open the walls of your mental house by a willingness to receive and weigh these thoughts in the balance of good judgment and to drop out of your mind everything except the one idea:

I want to know Truth, I am willing to learn. I want to express radiant health.

If there is not in your consciousness a demonstration that mind has a language on its own silent plane and that it can manifest itself in your mind, body, and affairs, then you can go back to your old convictions.

The fundamental basis and starting point of practical Christianity is that God is principle. By principle is meant definite, exact, and unchangeable rules of action. That the word *principle* is used by materialistic schools of thought to describe what they term the "blind forces of nature" is no reason why it should convey to our minds the idea of an unloving and unfeeling God. It is used because it best describes the unchangeableness that is an inherent law of Being.

From the teaching that the Deity is a person we have come to believe that God is changeable; that He gets angry with His people and condemns them; that some are chosen or favored above others; that in His sight good and evil are verities, and that He defends the one and deplores the other. We must relieve our minds of these ideas of a personal God ruling over us in an arbitrary, manlike manner.

God is mind. Mind evolves ideas. These ideas

are evolved in an orderly way. The laws of mind are just as exact and undeviating as the laws of mathematics or music. To recognize this is the starting point in finding God.

God loves spiritual man, and that love is expressed according to exact law. It is not emotional or variable, nor is there any taint of partiality in it. You are primarily a spiritual being, the expression of God's perfection, the receptacle of His love; and when you think and act in the consciousness of perfection and love, you cannot help being open to the influx of God's love and to the fulfillment of His divine purpose. This is the exact and undeviating law that inheres in the principle that God is.

God is wisdom; and wisdom is made manifest in an orderly manner through your consciousness.

God is substance—unchangeable incorruptible, imperishable—to the spiritual mind and body of man.

This substance of mind—faith—does not happen to be here today and there tomorrow, but it is moved upon by ideas which are as unchanging as Spirit.

In Spirit you never had a beginning, and your I AM will never have an ending. The world never had a beginning and will never have an ending. All things that are always were and always will be, yesterday, today, and forever the same.

But things formed have a beginning and may have an ending.

But God does not form things. God calls from the depths of His own being the ideas that are

already there, and they move forth and clothe themselves with the habiliments of time and circumstance
in man's consciousness. We must have firmly fixed in
our understanding the verity that we shall have
to square all the acts of life.

God is never absent from His creations, and His
creations are never absent from their habiliments;
hence wherever you see the evidences of life, there
you may know that God is.

If you are manifesting health, that health has a
source that is perpetually giving itself forth. A perpetual giving forth implies a perpetual presence.

There is no absence or separation in God. His
omnipresence is your omnipresence, because there
can be no absence in Mind. If God were for one instant separated from His creations, they would immediately fall into dissolution. But absence in Mind
is unthinkable. Mind is far removed from the realm
where time and distance prevail. Mind is without
metes or bounds; it is within all metes and bounds;
it does not exist but inheres in all that is. Hence in
spirit and in truth you can never for one instant be
separated from the life activity of God even though
you may not externally feel or know of His presence.

God lives in you, and you depend on Him for
every breath you draw. The understanding you have,
be it ever so meager, is from Him, and you could not
think a thought or speak a word or make a movement
were He not in it. Your body is the soil in which
God's life is planted. Your mind is the light for
which He supplies the oil. "I am the light of the

world," said Jesus. "Ye are the light of the world."

Intelligence is the light of the world. "Let your light shine." How? By increasing the supply of oil, by increasing your consciousness of life, and by learning how to draw upon the omnipresent God for every need.

A good healing drill is to deny the mental cause first, then the physical appearance. The mental condition should first be healed. Then the secondary state, which it has produced in the body, must be wiped out and the perfect state affirmed.

Deny:

I deny that I inherit any belief that in any way limits me in health, virtue, intelligence, or power to do good.

Those with whom I associate can no longer make me believe that I am a poor worm of the dust. The race belief that "nature dominates man" no longer holds me in bondage, and I am now free from every belief that might in any way interfere with my perfect expression of health, wealth, peace, prosperity, and perfect satisfaction in every department of life.

By my all-powerful word, in the sight and presence of almighty God, I now unformulate and destroy every foolish and ignorant assumption that might impede my march to perfection. My word is the measure of my power. I have spoken, and it shall be so.

Affirm:

I am unlimited in my power, and I have increasing health, strength, life, love, wisdom, boldness, freedom, charity, and meekness, now and forever.

I am now in harmony with the Father, and stronger than any mortal law. I know my birthright in pure Being, and I boldly assert my perfect freedom. In this knowledge I am enduring, pure, peaceful, and happy.

I am dignified and definite, yet meek and lowly, in all that I think and do.

I am one with and I now fully manifest vigorous life, wisdom, and spiritual understanding.

I am one with and I now fully manifest love, charity, justice, kindness, and generosity.

I am one with and I now fully manifest infinite goodness and mercy.

Peace floweth like a river through my mind, and I thank Thee, O God, that I am one with Thee!

CHAPTER III

Realization Precedes Manifestation

→»→»-«-«-

G OD'S MAN is hale, whole, hearty. This is Truth. A spiritual realization is a realization of Truth. A spiritual realization of health is the result of holding in consciousness a statement of health until the logic of the mind is satisfied and man receives the assurance that the fulfillment in the physical must follow. In other words, by realizing a healing prayer man lays hold of the principle of health itself and the whole consciousness is illumined; he perceives principle working out his health problems for him.

However when man lays hold of the principle of wholeness, he finds that he is automatically working with God and that much new power is added. He realizes: "My Father worketh even until now, and I work." After man has applied his mind diligently for a season, he exhausts his resources or powers of realization for the time being and rests from all his work; but his accumulated thought energy is completed or fulfilled in a higher realm, and he has a double assurance that health must become manifest.

Jesus understood and demonstrated this law perfectly. He was so much at one with the principle of health that He needed only to say, "Thy faith hath made thee whole" or "Lazarus, come forth,"

in order to bring into evidence the perfect demonstration.

Realization means at-one-ment, completion, perfection, wholeness, repose, resting in God. A realization of health brings to the consciousness an inner
knowing that the divine law has been fulfilled in
thought and act. Then as man lays hold of the indwelling Christ he is raised out of the Adam or
dark consciousness into the Christ consciousness. This
at-one-ment with God brings a lasting joy that cannot be taken away.

God-Mind rests in a perpetual realization of
health, and that which seems to be sickness does not
exist in Truth. When man becomes so much at one
with God-Mind that he abides in the consciousness
of health he enters the eternal peace in which he
knows that "it is finished."

In order to understand God-Mind we need to
study our own mind. The more we analyze the
processes of the mind the more plainly the mind
with its mental "compounds" appears as the source
of health and of all other things. In the realms of
dense matter intelligence may be so faint as to
have lost all contact with Mind. Yet the poet sings
about there being "sermons in stones." Again science
announces that life is present in and is disintegrating
the solid rocks and the whole earth groans and
creaks in her struggle with inertia. So if we want
to know the secrets of health and how right thinking
forms the perfect body, we must go to the mind and
trace step by step the movements that transform

ideas of health into light, electrons, atoms, molecules, cells, tissues, and finally into the perfect physical organism.

Although there is almost universal skepticism with reference to the mind's ability to know consciously how relative substance is formed, there are those who have made contact with the thought processes and can apply them in transforming the cells and tissues of their own body. The almost insurmountable obstacle to explaining to others how this is accomplished is the paucity of language. The mind functions in ways that are so strange and unbelievable that the pioneers on this frontier of metaphysics choose as a rule to remain silent.

Jesus is the outstanding pioneer in this realm where the health-producing processes of cells are released and imbued with supermind vitality.

He spent years in becoming acquainted with His body and freeing its cells from the material bondage to which the race thought had bound them.

Yet He gave no scientific explanation of the purifying through which He put His body to transform it before Peter, James, and John, as stated in Luke 9:29: "And as he was praying, the fashion of his countenance was altered, and his raiment *became* white *and* dazzling." Modern metaphysicians do not excuse their ignorance by claiming that this and many other instances in which Jesus showed mastery over His body were miracles. Scientific Christians regard as mortal superstition the prevalent view that miracles are the abrogation by God of His laws and are performed as a sort of legerdemain to attract and astonish the people. The marvelous things that Jesus did we can do when we understand the law. "The works that I do shall he do also; and greater" still holds good.

Much that is attributed to the subconscious, strictly speaking, springs from the all-knowing or spiritual Mind. When we cannot intellectually account for our knowledge we assume the subconscious to be its source. Yet we should know that the subconscious is the storehouse of past knowledge and past experiences. So it knows only what has filtered through the conscious mind. It cannot therefore be the source of knowledge except through reflection or memory. This memory of what man has passed through in the aeons of his experience is often called intuition; it is the instinct of the animal soul.

The world today looks up to science; that is, it does not accept or believe anything unless it can be demonstrated by well-known universal laws. There are no known laws governing religion that can be scientifically explained; hence it is not acceptable to the scientific mind. But there is a technique for molding thought stuff by means of the mind, and metaphysicians follow it in their scientific thinking and in healing. The metaphysician handles omnipresent Spirit life and substance very much as the electrician handles electricity. Energy is locked up in all this life and substance and its release enables the metaphysician to utilize it in demonstrating health and in achieving success.

All the chemical elements adhere to their particular form and endeavor to retain it. Electricity is supposed to be a universal invisible energy whose unity can be broken up by the whirl of a dynamo. The electronic units exert all the force of their nature in a pull to regain their original status. Thus the power generated by a dynamo is gained from the force exerted by the electrical units in their rush to establish their primal equipoise.

Only a certain percentage of this energy is utilized because of the pull of the electrical units to get back home to their mother principle. The dissipation of energy is one of the great problems of the engineer. The loss of electricity in transmission is so great that only a small part of the original current reaches its destination.

We exist right in the midst of forces that would yield us power to do all our work if we knew how to conserve and properly utilize their energies. This is not only true of our use of the many elements in the natural world all about us but especially of our utilization of the energy generated by our minds. If we could utilize this dissipated energy constructively it would restore the body, illumine the mind, and establish us in a lasting consciousness of dominion and mastery.

With every thought there is a radiation of energy. If a person is untrained in thinking and lets his mind express all kinds of thoughts without control, he not only uses up his thought stuff but fails also to accomplish any helpful result.

Conservation of thought stuff is essential to right thinking. Right thinking is using the mind to bring about right ends idealized by the thinker. All the elements necessary to the restoration of health exist in the higher dimensions of the mind. Through concentration and conservation of thought force man regains the consciousness of health in his mind, and health then becomes manifest in his body.

Laws fixed by infinite Mind automatically accomplish whatever man desires when he becomes obedient to the inner guide. Concentration, one-pointed attention, forms a mental magnet in the mind to which thought substance rushes like iron filings to a loadstone. Then follows confidence or faith in one's ability to accomplish the desired end. According to the Scriptures this is the law by which the universe was brought into manifestation. In the 11th chapter of Hebrews it is written: "By faith we understand that the worlds have been framed by the word of God."

Modern science by its most daring proponents is launching out into the deeps of the invisible and describing in detail the electrical processes that ultimate in the atom and its aggregations in visible things. In substance they tell us that when points of light gather about a certain nucleus an atom is created, and from this a cell, and cell aggregations make tissues and these merge into the realm of things.

Here we have the scientific explanation and the Christian metaphysician's formula for making the invisible visible. The greatest of all physicists cannot tell what electricity is. Even Edison said he was ignorant of its real nature. Some find it sometimes acting very much like mind and have so stated. The head of the General Electric research department was asked by a reporter to give him a definition of electricity. The professor replied that to his mind electricity was like what the Christians describe as faith.

The scientific metaphysician fixes his attention powerfully on the consummation of a certain idea until he has a realization, which means that the idea has nucleated a certain amount of thought substance. When this realization is had the metaphysician rests "from all his work." Through faith and work he has fulfilled the law of mind and he rests in the conviction that his ideal of health will appear in manifestation in due season.

To a metaphysician realization is the conviction that a person gets when he has persistently concentrated his attention on an ideal until he feels assured of the fulfillment of that ideal. Elohim God pronounced His spiritual creation "very good"; then rested from all His work. There was as yet no manifestation, "no herb of the field had yet sprung up," and "there was not a man to till the ground"; yet the planning Mind had the realization that the spiritual law had been fulfilled and that it should rest from all its works.

That all things visible are held in place by a force invisible is the conviction of the majority of logical thinkers. In other words, everything is ensouled. When we understand that the soul has consciousness, that it thinks, we have the explanation of many mysterious phenomena. Some 150 years ago Franz Mesmer announced in Germany that under certain conditions he could induce a magnetic sleep in persons and control their minds. His demonstrations attracted the attention of doctors and mental scientists the world over. In this day the system is practiced under the name of hypnotism. It is full of pitfalls for both operator and patient because its tendency is to weaken the positive control that the mind should always exercise over its own brain structure. However it is one of the many proofs that the mind can produce conditions in the mental world that ultimate in the material world. A great physical scientist stated recently that it may be that the gods that determine our fates are our own minds working on our brain cells and through them on the world about us. This is very close to the Truth.

Every Christian metaphysician knows that back of the personal mind there is a great creative Mind that also recreates. This creative Mind has been named and described by men all down the ages. God-Mind not only can restore and heal but can establish us in the consciousness of permanent health. Do not allow your conception of God to be handicapped by what men have said about Him.

"There is a spirit in man,

   And the breath of the Almighty giveth them understanding."

Let the Spirit of God in you reveal to you His true

character. God was never sick a day; He is the source of life and health and joy. God wills that we express His "image" and "likeness," in which we were created.

The prayer for realization attains its consummation when with concentrated spiritual attention one has affirmed that God Spirit is present, that with all His power He is bringing to pass the perfect health desired, and that all is well. When your thoughts radiate with the speed of spiritual light, they blend with creative Mind (called by Jesus "heaven"), and the thing you have asked for will be done. Jesus told Peter that whatever he bound (affirmed) in earth would be bound in heaven and whatever he loosed (denied) in earth would be loosed in heaven. Peter had unbounded faith in Jesus (who represents spiritual man). When any man has unbounded faith in spiritual power his words, uttered in the limitations of matter, are flashed to heaven (creative Mind) and they accomplish whatever he puts into them. The fulfillment of this spoken word in the world of activities may take moments, hours, days, years, centuries; Jesus said that the Father only knew when these things would come to pass. Do not think because you do not get an instant response to your prayers that they are not answered. Every sincere desire and every effectual prayer for health that has ascended to heaven (creative Mind) is fulfilled, and will be made manifest whenever material limitations permit. Shakespeare had an inkling of this law of the relation of thoughts and words when he wrote,

"My words fly up, my thoughts remain below:
Words without thoughts never to heaven go."

The kingdom of heaven (the heavens) so often
referred to by Jesus and described by Him as very
near to us is far more accessible and is more often
contacted by us than we imagine. Not only those
who pray but those who persistently concentrate
their thoughts on mathematics, music, or philoso-
phies based in principle, are often rewarded with the
marvelous intuitions of genius. These persons apparently break into a realm where no effort is required to gain the answer to their questions. The
mathematical genius is called a prodigy. He solves
instantly the most complex mathematical problem,
yet cannot explain how he does it. He simply knows
the answer, often before the statement of the problem has been completed.

Henri Poincaré in his book "Science and Method" says that his discoveries in mathematics came
to him in flashes after he had spent long periods of
study and concentration on the subject. Concentrated
attention of the mind on an idea of any kind is equal
to prayer and will make available the spiritual principle that is its source in proportion to the intensity
and continuity of the mental effort. Anyone can
attain spiritual understanding and become conscious
of the light who will persistently pray for it. "He
that cometh to God must believe that he is, and *that*
he is a rewarder of them that diligently seek him."
The emphasis here is on the word "diligently."

The mind is the seat of perfection, not only of health but also of talents like music, art, writing, and the like. The idea of health and the idea of music are interblended, for instance. Music is a great aid to the healing force. Musical and health ideas interblend, and their establishment in order produces this kingdom of the heavens.

Our spiritual realizations produce that silent shuttle of thought which, working in and through cell and nerve, weaves into one harmonious whole mind and body and is expressed as health and wealth and genius.

The musical genius says he hears the music in a flash and is often at his wit's end to transcribe it fast enough. Many an immortal poem and prose work as well has been flashed from the mind of the author without any apparent effort on his part. But if all the prayers and mind efforts of literary geniuses were inquired into, it would be found that there had been heroic mental effort somewhere at some time. So it is with healing. The realization of perfection takes root in the soul and may come forth in a flash as perfect health. We should not confine ourselves to the present life of the individual but go into previous incarnations in which the work was done that made the genius in this incarnation.

Professor Einstein was considered the greatest mathematical genius of our time. The scientific world does not connect his insight into scientific principles with his religious life, but he freely stated that he worshiped God. He said: "The voice of God is from within. Something within me tells me what I must do every day." For him God is as valid as a scientific argument. On the subject of spiritual realization he once said:

"Every man knows that in his work he does best and accomplishes most when he has attained a proficiency that enables him to work intuitively. That is, there are things that we come to know so well that we do not know how we know them. Perhaps we live best and do things best when we are not too conscious of how and why we do them."

The supreme realization of man is his unity with God. Jesus had this realization and proclaimed it before there was any manifestation. When He told His followers, "I and the Father are one" and "He that hath seen me hath seen the Father," they demanded that He show them the Father. They could not then understand that He had spiritually united with creative Mind. Men in our day are having this realization in a more universal way than ever before in the history of the race, and they are affirming it in the face of ridicule and condemnation. When this inner consciousness is attained by any man the foundation has been laid of the Peter church or temple that is man's immortal body, which will never pass away.

Metaphysically realization is expectancy objectified. The mind conceives a proposition and then marshals all its forces to make that conception a reality in the objective world. All things material are first thought pictures, carved by the imagina-

tion from omnipresent thought substance. Shakespeare in "Much Ado about Nothing" brings out
the idea as follows:

> The idea of her life shall sweetly creep
> Into his study of imagination,
> And every lovely organ of her life,
> Shall come appareled in more precious habit,
> More moving-delicate and full of life
> Into the eye and prospect of his soul.

This realm of realization is so real to the mind
that it requires a trained metaphysician to detect
the difference between its creations and the manifest realm of things. We all have a body in the ether
that is the counterpart of the physical. It is through
this psychic body that we have sensation in the
physical. It is possible to think of the psychic body
and cultivate its sensations until it appears as real
as the physical. Many persons have done this until
they have formed a psychic world consciousness
and they are often unable to separate it from the
physical. They search materially for the treasures
they see psychically. To them the realm of thought
forms is the finality of creation instead of the mental
pictures of that which is about to appear.

The trained metaphysician is no stranger to this
picture gallery of the mind and he is not deceived
into believing that it is any more than a mental reflection. One who enters the realm of spiritual ideas
does not allow his consciousness to become con-
fused with the mind pictures that flash into psychic
sight. They are part of the process of making ideas
manifest. When a Christian healer realizes that his

treatment has firmly formed the picture of health, he relaxes his decrees and statements of Truth and trusts the divine law to make health manifest.

Paul urges in many of his writings that we have the Mind of Christ: that we let Christ be formed in us. This has usually been taken to mean that we are to imitate Christ. This is good as far as it goes, but it does not go far enough. To follow Jesus Christ in the regeneration or new birth we must fulfill the law of body building, which is a reconstruction of the corrupt cells: "This corruptible must put on incorruption." To accomplish this and make the body conform to His perfect body we must see Him as He is in His perfect body. This perfect body exists as an ideal body in us all. By mentally concentrating on this perfect body and focusing all our powers on it as the vital life of the physical a transformation will begin that will finally raise the physical to divine stature. Paul points the way in II Corinthians:

"But we all, with unveiled face beholding as in a mirror the glory of the Lord, are transformed into the same image from glory to glory, even as from the Lord the Spirit."

CHAPTER IV

Producing Results

->>>->>> <<<-<<<-

I T IS A striking fact that even back in the time of Moses the health of the people was considered of great importance and was always mentioned in connection with their spiritual welfare. If they were obedient to the law, they kept in health; if disobedient, they fell sick. The same law that brought about these results has always been operative and is active in our midst today. Faith in God as the health of His people and obedience to the law of Being bring health. Distrust and disobedience produce ill-health.

It has been proved again and again that there is a definite relation between the thoughts of man and the conditions in his body. Scientists of the world are experimenting with mental processes and are discovering that the old Scripture writers knew whereof they spoke when they taught that sin produces sickness and righteousness health. It is known that infants have been poisoned by the milk from the breasts of angry mothers. Persons under the stress of fear suffer a loss of appetite. Many other illustrations of the effect of discordant mental states come to those who study mind and its manifestations. Job understood the relation between a mental concept and its result. He said: "The thing which I fear cometh upon me."

In the past century there has been a general awakening among people to the realization of the relation between righteousness and health, and men everywhere are seeking the knowledge of God and His healing power. God becomes to them their "all-sufficiency in everything." This all-sufficiency manifests itself to them according to their needs. To one it is health, to another it is freedom from bondage to some habit, to a third person it is illumination.

Jesus was the great teacher and example of obedience to the law of constructive thinking. All His commandments and sayings tend toward the enhancement of life and health and harmony. The reforms that man in mortal consciousness tries to make are all based on destructive ideas set to work in the external. The reform of Jesus is an inner transformation: "I am not come to destroy, but to fulfill." He came not to tear down but to build up. If we follow Him we shall give our strength and substance and thought force to constructive activity.

In order to understand the Scriptures and especially the portion of them that gives the life and experiences of Jesus it is necessary to study the action of the mind. The movement of every mind in bringing forth the simplest thought is a key to the great creative process of universal Mind. In every act is involved mind, idea, and manifestation. The mind is neither seen nor felt; the idea is not seen, but it is felt; and the manifestation appears.

The history of mankind in the majority of its aspects shows a steady growth or ascent from a lower to a higher estate. In the forms of nature external to man the same law of development is seen. Jesus' statement that "the earth beareth fruit of herself; first the blade, then the ear, then the full grain in the ear" is a recognition of the truth that evolution in the earth is universal.

The progress of man through the aid of uplifting influences has been especially marked in the education of the mind. In the field of mathematics alone almost unbelievable increase in the understanding of abstract truth has been gained over a period that began with the crude though systematic work of the Egyptians, about 2500 B.C., and extended to include the seventeenth-century research of Leibnitz, who developed the branch of higher mathematics known as the infinitesimal calculus.

Steady progress has been the rule also in that phase of life which deals with a man's relations to his fellow men. The various activities of social service have led to improved working conditions, better homes, and more helpful environments for those whose condition of life has called for the help of their brothers. Sociology has thus resulted in many movements for the uplift of mankind.

In the field of religion the upward march has been especially remarkable. There is a wide range of religious experience between the blindly groping faith that caused men to pass their children through the fire as sacrifices to their deities and the divine consciousness of Jesus Christ, who submitted His body to the purifying fire of the Spirit and came forth alive with a life that never dies.

The healing of the body of man must follow the law of evolution, in common with the education of his mind and the adjustment of his social relations. Jesus did His healing spiritually. When He was told of the "great fever" of Simon's mother-in-law, He administered no drug to reduce her temperature. Instead He "stood over her, and rebuked the fever; and it left her." Jesus knew the law that "without any dispute the less is blessed by the better." He knew that the blessing of health comes through the exercise of faith on the part of the man who seeks it, that faith opens the mind to the influx of power from on high, and that the power of the Highest heals all diseases both of soul and of body.

When faith is sufficiently strong to dissolve all adverse conditions and to open the mind fully to the power of God, healing is instantaneous. In the natural course of events the patient who survives a fever goes through a long, slow convalescence; hence perhaps the name "patient." Jesus had no "patients" although He healed many who were "sick with divers diseases." Simon's mother-in-law rose up immediately and went about her work when Jesus denied the power of the fever to hold her.

After a busy day of teaching in the synagogue in the course of which Jesus restored to his right mind a man who "had a spirit of an unclean demon," He ended the evening by healing, without exception, "every one of them" that were brought to Him. He had spent no time in the study of pathology prior to this work. Shortly before that time He had spent forty days in the wilderness in communion with God and in setting His own purposes in order by the light of the divine understanding that He had gained there. After each season of healing and intensive teaching He again withdrew into a desert place or to a mountain, either alone or in company with His apostles, and there obtained a new influx of power from the Father. So the healing work went on. There is no record of incurables.

Further there is no record that Jesus took any precautions to avoid infection when He was engaged in healing the sick. He was without fear of evil because He acknowledged only the power of the Highest, which is good. He put His hand on the leper to prove to him that He was fearless and confident. He spoke six short, decisive words, "I will; be thou made clean"; and we are told that "straightway his leprosy was cleansed" although the Scripture shows that he was in the last stage of the disease ("full of leprosy"). There were no long explanations, no instructions given. Jesus simply turned His super-will upon the leper, and the power of the Highest flowed through Him instantly to do its perfect work. Then only did an instruction follow. The leper was told to offer the usual praise and sacrifice to God and to ascribe his healing to the Highest rather than to the power of personality.

Jesus always connected sin and sickness as cause and effect. When the man sick of the palsy was let down through the roof of a house that he might be brought before Jesus for healing, there were those present who expected the healing to be done in some mysterious way; and when Jesus spoke of forgiving the man's sins in order to heal him they said: "Who is this that speaketh blasphemies? Who can forgive sins, but God alone?" These men lived in a material world and saw everything from a material viewpoint. They did not understand that the man's sins caused his palsy. As a proof of man's power to forgive sin and thus heal the effects of sin Jesus said when the man was brought for healing:

"But that ye may know that the Son of man hath authority on earth to forgive sins (he said unto him that was palsied), I say unto thee, Arise, and take up thy couch, and go unto thy house. And immediately he rose up before them, and took up that whereon he lay, and departed to his house, glorifying God."

Jesus taught plainly that the mind was the place of origin of every act. He said that if there was lust in the heart, it was sin even though no overt act were committed. All thinking people in this day accept without question the fact that the body is moved by the mind; and those who have made a study of mental processes have found that all the conditions of the body are brought about by the mind; also that there is a law of right thought and that a departure from that law is sin or "missing one's aim," which is the original Hebrew conception of sin.

Forgiveness really means the giving up of something. When you forgive yourself, you cease doing the thing that you ought not to do. Jesus was correct in assuming that man has power to forgive sin. Sin is a falling short of the divine law, and repentance and forgiveness are the only means that man has of getting out of sin and its effect and coming into harmony with the law. But who can tell what the law is? Only those who study man as a spiritual and mental being. Study of manifestation alone is futile; it leads nowhere. We must get at it from the cause side. All sin is first in the mind; and the forgiveness is a change of mind or repentance. Some mental attitude, some train of mental energy, must be transformed. We forgive sin in ourselves every time we resolve to think and act according to the divine law. The mind must change from a material to a spiritual base. The law is already fixed; there is nothing in it to be changed, because God is the lawgiver and does not change. The change must all be on the part of man and within him. The moment man changes his thoughts of sickness to thoughts of health the divine law rushes in and begins the healing work.

The law is Truth, and the Truth is that all is good. There is no power and no reality in sin. If sin were real and enduring, like goodness and Truth, it could not be forgiven but would hold its victim forever. When we enter into the understanding of the real and the unreal, a great light dawns upon us and we see what Jesus meant when He said, "The Son of man hath authority on earth to forgive sins." The Son of man is that in us which discerns the difference between Truth and error. When we get this understanding, we are in a position to free our soul from sin and our body from disease, which is the effect of sin. Sin is the result of desire manifesting itself in erroneous ways and may be compared to the errors of the child working a problem in mathematics. When the error is discovered and there is a willingness to correct it, under the law of forgiveness man erases it as easily as the child rubs out the false figures in his exercise. Thus in spiritual understanding, the I AM of man forgives or "gives" Truth "for" error; the mind is set in order and the body healed. The moment man realizes this he puts himself in harmony with the Truth of Being, and the law wipes out all his transgressions.

In denying the reality of sin send out your freeing thought to others as well as to yourself. Do not hold anyone in bondage to the thought of sin. If you do, it will pile up and increase in power according to the laws of mental action.

No one can understand how forgiveness sets free the sin-bound soul and the sick body unless he studies mind and has some understanding of its laws. There is a universal thought substance in which thought builds whatever man wills.

The right images become active through the power of thought. Man has unlimited power through thought, and he can give his power to things or withhold it. If he thinks about the power of sin, he builds up and gives force to that belief until it engulfs him in its whirlpool of thought substance. He forgets his spiritual origin and sees only the human.

He thinks of himself as a sinner "born in sin and conceived in iniquity" rather than as the image and likeness of God.

Man also sees the law of sowing and reaping, and he fears his sins and their results. Then fear of the divine law is added to his burdens. The way out of this maze of ignorance, sin, and sickness is through man's understanding of his real being, and then the forgiving or the giving up of all thoughts of the reality of sin and its effects in the body.

But we must recognize the unity of the race in Christ and include all people in our forgiving. A good freeing statement is:

"I do not believe in the power of sin in myself or in others."

If anyone tries to free himself while holding others in the thought of sin, he will not demonstrate his freedom. No man can rise except as he lifts the race with him in his thought: "and I, if I be lifted up from the earth, will draw all men unto myself." As by one man sin came into the world so by one man it is taken away. As all were included in the sin of one so all are included in the righteousness of one, and every man stands sinless before God in Christ. Recognition of this will make men free, and the greater the number of men that recognize and declare the Truth the sooner will all men know that they are free from sin in Christ.

You must build upon faith in the reality of the spiritual. The next step is to put your selfishness away. There cannot be two in this kingdom. It is the kingdom of God, and man must give up. The John the Baptist must recognize the Son of God that is in you and that this Son must be always active in you in love, life, and power. The kingdom is for the larger man. The personal man must be eliminated.

The next step is love, universal love: not the love of earthly possessions but the love of spiritual things. We must give up the flesh man and all his possessions and at the same time lay hold of the spiritual man. Then we have everything although apparently we may have nothing. This is a difficult proposition to those who think in terms of material ideas. You must be able to get away from all thought of material things. "Love . . . seeketh not its own"; "is not puffed up." Love is not selfish. We cannot have selfishness and love at the same time. We cannot have this universal brotherhood unless we love everybody. We must love all because we are all one. There must be in our consciousness a recognition of the universal right of all to all the possessions of the world.

Then there must be this inner growth that is a fuller consciousness of the new life which comes with the entering into this kingdom of Christ.

The fact is that there is a foundation for this world-wide movement in behalf of purer men and better things for all. There is something back of it all, and the old conditions, diseases, and limitations must pass away; and the time is now ripe for entering into this kingdom, this attainment of the spiritual side of life, this growing of a new body; and every one of us can enter in if we only will to do so.

True, in all actual transformation of mind and body a dissolving, breaking-up process necessarily takes place, because thought force and substance have been built into the errors that appear. In each individual these errors have the power that man has given to them by his thought concerning them. These thought structures must be broken up and eliminated from consciousness. The simplest, most direct, and most effective method is to withdraw from them the life and substance that have been going to feed them, and to let them shrivel away into their own nothingness. This withdrawal is best accomplished by denial of the power and reality of evil and affirmation of the allness of Spirit. Nothing is destroyed, because "nothing" can't be destroyed. The change that takes place is merely a transference of power from an error belief to faith in the Truth, through the recognition that God is good and is all that in reality exists.

The doctrine of the Trinity is often a stumbling block, because we find it difficult to understand how three persons can be one. Three persons cannot be one, and theology will always be a mystery until theologians become metaphysicians. It is necessary to understand the Trinity in order to be healed in soul and body.

God is the name of the all-encompassing Mind. Christ is the name of the all-loving Mind. Holy Spirit is the all-active manifestation. These three are one fundamental Mind in its three creative aspects.

We have to be healed physically, mentally, and

spiritually. Often people think they are sick physically when they are just sick in soul. It is easy to
understand how the idea of perfect health may exist
in the great Father-Mind; also how that idea may
become active in the individual and manifest in his
life. This simple comparison clears up the mystery
of the Trinity. Here are the Scripture symbols compared with modern metaphysical terms:

God—Christ—man.
Mind—idea—manifestation.
Father—Son—Holy Spirit.
Thinker—thought—action.
Spirit—soul—body.
I AM—I AM conscious—I appear.

We want the actual overcoming power of Christ.
To get this we must appreciate life and enter into it
thankfully and heartily. "I came that they may have
life, and may have *it* abundantly." This abundant
life is always present. When we recognize it and
open our consciousness to it, it comes flowing into
mind and body with its mighty quickening, healing
power, and they are renewed and transformed.

The following affirmations are for the purpose
of establishing the whole man in the consciousness
of unity and health. They are given as they came
into mind without any attempt at classification:

*My body does not starve for my love and appre-
ciation of it. I recognize it, honor it, and love it as
the body temple of the living God.*

*I have now the only body I ever had. Though
I were reincarnated a thousand times, yet is my body*

*the same. It is I. Its appearance depends on my be-
liefs and thoughts and changes accordingly, but it is
always the same body, even as my soul and spirit
are always the same. My body is as much a part of
my individuality as my soul. It is eternal, like any
other part of my I. It is I, even as my soul is I.*

*I cannot disown my body and say that I borrowed
it from my parents. This is not the truth. I may have
taken up some of my parents' error beliefs and built
them into my body; but my body came from no one
but God. It came from Him with my spirit and soul
and has ever coexisted with them. These three are
one, inseparable. It is the belief in man that his body
is separate from him and is something that he merely
owns that makes the appearance of separation. I do
not own my body: I am body. I do not own my soul:
I am soul. I do not own my spirit: I am spirit. And
these three are one.*

*The redemption of the body depends on my hav-
ing the right idea of body. It must be the divine idea,
and there must be no other. The eye must be single.*

*My body (or I manifested as body) is not filled
with error, sin, discord. Beholding myself free from
these keeps me manifesting thus. The law of growth
is in beholding. While I behold the body as anything
else but its divine idea I hold it there. It can never
change before the belief of it changes.*

*I am. I am in every cell of my body. I am every
cell of my body. I do not disown my body. I do not
withdraw my I, but I take possession—full possession
—of every part in the name of the Lord.*

I now fully identify myself with my body even as with my soul and spirit, thus making the at-one-ment.

Since my body is I, if there appears resistance in it, that resistance is my own; it comes only from me. It comes from my failure properly to identify myself with my body. The way to get control is to take it. This I do, not by will power, by personal force, or by anything that recognizes my body as separate from me, but by my consciousness of oneness with it. This unifies all of me and stops all resistance.

My body is life, purity, wholeness, sinlessness. In my flesh I see God. What I see, what I behold, becomes manifest.

"Beloved, believe not every spirit, but prove the spirits, whether they are of God; because many false prophets are gone out into the world. Hereby know ye the Spirit of God: every spirit that confesseth that Jesus Christ is come in the flesh is of God: and every spirit that confesseth not Jesus is not of God."

I confess that Jesus Christ is come in the flesh, even in my flesh.

"Not for that we would be unclothed, but that we would be clothed upon, that what is mortal may be swallowed up of life."

The idea of the body as an earthly house is now dissolved, and I am now clothed upon with the heavenly house, even the divine idea of man complete. In this idea I am one with the immortal, incorruptible flesh of Jesus Christ, and I have eternal life. I do confess that Jesus Christ is come in the flesh.

CHAPTER V

The Omnipotence of Prayer

->>>->>><<<-<<<-

TO A PERSON in the understanding of Truth prayer should be an affirmation of that which is in Being.

What is the necessity of the prayer of affirmation if Being already is? In order that the creative law of the Word may be fulfilled. All things are in God as potentialities. It is man's office under the divine law to bring into manifestation that which has been created or planned by the unmanifest. Everybody should pray. Through prayer we develop the highest phase of character. Prayer softens and refines the whole man. A prominent skeptic once said that the most unattractive thing in existence was a prayerless woman.

Prayer is not supplication or begging but a simple asking for that which we know is waiting for us at the hands of our Father and an affirmation of its existence. The prayer that Jesus gave as a model is simplicity itself. There is none of that awe-inspiring "O Thou" that ministers often affect in public prayer but only the ordinary informal request of a son to his Father for things needed.

"Father . . . Hallowed be thy name." Here in the Lord's Prayer is a recognition of the all-inclusiveness and completeness of Divine Mind. Everything has its sustenance from this one source; therefore "the

67

earth is the Lord's, and the fulness thereof."

We need supplies for the day only. Hoarding for future necessity breeds selfishness. The Children of Israel tried to save the manna, but it spoiled on their hands.

The law "Whatsoever a man soweth, that shall he also reap" is here shorn of its terrors. If we forgive others we shall be forgiven, and the penalty of suffering for sins will be eliminated.

It does not seem possible that God would lead us into temptation. The statement about temptation follows closely that regarding the forgiveness of sin, and it is evidently a part of it. "Let not temptation lead us" is a permissible interpretation.

Jesus advised asking for what we want and being persistent in our demands. People ignorant of the relation in which man stands to God wonder why we should ask and even importune a Father who has provided all things for us. This is explained when we perceive that God is a great mind reservoir that has to be tapped by man's mind and poured into visibility through man's thought or word. If the mind of man is clogged with doubt, lethargy, or fear, he must open the way by persistent knocking and asking. "Pray without ceasing," "continuing instant in prayer." Acquire in prayer a facility in asking equal to the mathematician's expertness in handling numbers and you will get responses in proportion.

We give our children what we consider good gifts from our limited and transitory store, but when the gifts of God are put into our minds we have possessions that are eternal and will go on being productive for all time.

Undoubtedly the one thing that stands out prominently in the teaching of Jesus is the necessity of prayer. He prayed on the slightest pretext, or in some such manner invoked the presence of God. He prayed over situations that most men would deal with without the intervention of God. If He was verily God incarnate, the skeptic often asks, why did He so often appeal to an apparently higher God. To answer this doubt intelligently and truly one must understand the constitution of man.

There are always two men in each individual. The man without is the picture that the man within paints with his mind. This mind is the open door to the unlimited principle of Being. When Jesus prayed He was setting into action the various powers of His individuality in order to bring about certain results. Within His identity was of God; without He was human personality.

The various mental attitudes denoted by the word prayer are not comprehended by those unfamiliar with the spiritual consititution of man. When the trained metaphysician speaks of his demonstrations through prayer, he does not explain all the movements of his spirit and mind, because the outer consciousness has not the capacity to receive it.

When we read of Jesus spending whole nights in prayer, the first thought is that He was asking and begging God for something. But we find prayer to be many-sided; it is not only asking but receiving also. We must pray believing that we shall receive. Prayer is both invocation and affirmation. Meditation, concentration, denial, and affirmation in the silence are all forms of what is loosely termed prayer.

Thus Jesus was demonstrating at night over the error thoughts of mind. He was lifting the mortal mind up to the plane of Spirit through some prayerful thought. The Son of man must be lifted up, and there is no way to do this except through prayer.

One who exercises his thought powers discovers that there is a steady growth with proper use. The powers of the mind are developed in much the same way that the muscles of the body are. Persistent affirmation of a certain desire in the silence concentrates the mental energies and beats down all barriers.

Jesus illustrates the power of such affirmative prayer, of repeated silent demands for justice, for instance, by the case of the widow bereft of worldly protection and power. To the widow's persistence even the ungodly judge succumbs. The unceasing prayer of faith is commanded in the Scriptures in various places.

If a man's prayers are based on the thought of his own righteousness and the sinfulness of others, he does not fulfill the law of true prayer. Self-righteousness is an exclusory thought and closes the door to the great Father love that we all want. We are not to justify ourselves in the sight of God but let the Spirit of justice and righteousness do its perfect work through us.

That God and angels and heaven exist is accepted by all who believe the Scriptures, but there is wide diversity of thought about their character and abode. Those who read the Bible after the letter have invented all kinds of imaginary notions as to the conditions under which God and His angels live and as to the location of heaven. Their minds being fixed on things, they have not conceived of the realm of ideas, and they are therefore totally ignorant of the true teaching of the Scriptures. To understand the Bible one must know about the constitution of man. This is the key to all mysteries, the knowledge of man's true self. "Know thyself."

Man is spirit, soul, body. These are coexistent. God is the principle of being as an axiom is a principle of mathematics. God is not confined to locality. Is a mathematical principle confined to a particular place and not found elsewhere? "The kingdom of God is within you." God is the real of man's being. It follows that all the powers that are attributed to God may become operative in man. Then we live right in the presence of God and angels and heaven. What seems a desert place is filled with angelic messengers, and like Jacob we know it not.

Man sets into action any of the three realms of his being, spirit, soul, and body, by concentrating his thought on them. If he thinks only of the body, the physical senses encompass all his existence. If mind and emotion are cultivated he adds soul to his consciousness. If he rises to the Absolute and comprehends Spirit, he rounds out the God-man.

Spirit is the source of soul and body, hence the

ruling power. Its works are so swift and so transcend the limitations of matter that the natural man cannot comprehend them and hence calls them "miracles." But all things are done under law. "Prayer was made earnestly of the church unto God for him," and Peter was delivered from prison by an angel. The earnest prayers of the devout believers in the power of supreme Spirit brought about the result. The history of Christianity is full of instances of so-called miracles wrought through prayer. The hour-long prayer of Luther by what was supposed to be the deathbed of his friend Melanchthon is a famous instance of importunate pleadings. It was Luther's firm belief that Melanchthon's years of continued life were the direct answer to his prayers.

Mighty things have been wrought in the past by those who had mere blind faith to guide them. To faith we now add understanding of the law, and our achievements will be a fulfillment of the promise of Jesus "He that believeth on me, the works that I do shall he do also; and greater *works* than these shall he do." The prayer of Luther and its results are now being duplicated every day. As we go on in the exercise of the spiritual faculties we shall strengthen them and understand them better, and we shall cease to talk about anything miraculous. All things are possible to man when he exercises his spiritual power under the divine law.

When man directs the power of exalted ideas into his body, he exalts the cells, releases their innate spiritual energy, and causes them finally to disappear from physical sight into the omnipresent luminous ether. This is what Jesus accomplished at His ascension. The promise was that all who follow Him in the regeneration of the body would do likewise. It is true that even the followers of Jesus have not always understood the scientific import of His doctrine. They have mentally absorbed His exalted ideas and looked to their fulfillment in a faraway heaven in the skies. By thus projecting their ideas toward a fulfillment outside of the body they have separated their soul or mind consciousness from its companion, the body, and the deserted cells have been resolved into their mother principle, the earth.

The mind of man is constantly projecting thought energies or waves through brain cells into the ether or space element in which we live. Every person lives in an environment of radiant energy that circulates through the cells of his organism like bees in a hive. Ordinarily we cannot see the radiations of the mind, but we almost universally feel them. When a discordant mind impinges upon our mind radiations we instinctively shrink away. But we are radiantly happy in the presence of an exalted mind.

"No man hath beheld God at any time." Seers, prophets, preachers, and holy men and women in all ages are a unit in saying that they have become acquainted with God through prayer, expressed in the spirit of their minds.

This testimony to God's spiritual presence is so unanimous that no one seeks His help in any way other than through the spirit of the mind; and the fact that we know God with our minds and not with our senses proves that God is Spirit.

In its higher functioning the mind of man deals with spiritual ideas, and we can truthfully say that man is a spiritual being. This fact explains the almost universal worship of God by men and makes possible the conjunction of the heaven and the earth by those who understand the underlying laws of prayer. Jesus stated this emphatically in John 4:24 (margin): "God is Spirit; and they that worship him must worship in spirit and truth."

Then the real foundation of all effective prayer is the understanding that God is Spirit and that man, His offspring, is His image and likeness, hence spiritual.

Such a concept of God gives man a point of contact that is never absent; in all places and under all conditions he has the assurance of the attention and help of God when he realizes the Father's spiritual presence and comradeship.

When it has a spiritually poised mind to work through, Spirit is not limited in its power by any material environment. "With God all things are possible." To make this strong statement of Jesus come true we must study the laws of God and strive to carry them out through a quickened consciousness.

The Bible is replete with situations where men and women seemed beyond any material help, but through faith and prayer they triumphed right in the face of seemingly insurmountable obstacles. The author of the 11th chapter of Hebrews builds pyramids of faith demonstrations. Hear the climax:

"And what shall I more say? for the time will fail me if I tell of Gideon, Barak, Samson, Jephthah; of David and Samuel and the prophets who through faith subdued kingdoms, wrought righteousness, obtained promises, stopped the mouths of lions, quenched the power of fire, escaped the edge of the sword, from weakness were made strong, waxed mighty in war, turned to flight armies of aliens."

Paul might have added to his pyramid of faith the long list of miraculous healings of diseases and many superhuman works recorded in the Bible, among which are the restoration of the leper Naaman and the resurrection of the Shunammite's son by Elisha; the control of the elements by Elijah; the overcoming of gravity in the floating of the workman's axhead from the bottom of the Jordan by Elisha, and Moses' causing the water to gush from the rock.

The majority of people think that great spiritual faith is necessary to get marvelous results. But Jesus taught differently. "The apostles said unto the Lord, Increase our faith. And the Lord said, If ye had faith as a grain of mustard seed, ye would say unto this sycamine tree, Be thou rooted up, and be thou planted in the sea; and it would obey you."

The mustard is among the smallest of seeds, and the comparison would indicate what a tiny bit of real faith is necessary to cause motion in material things. Paul and Silas in the Roman jail prayed and sang until their bonds fell off, the doors flew open, and they walked out, both free men. On the day of Pentecost the followers of Jesus prayed and sang until the ethers were so accelerated that tongues of fire flashed from the bodies of the worshipers, and they were miraculously quickened in mental ability.

Prayer liberates the energies pent up in mind and body. Those who pray much create a spiritual aura that eventually envelops the whole body. The bands of light painted by artists around the heads of saints are not imaginary; they actually exist and are visible to the sharp eye of the painter. The Scriptures testify in Luke 9:29 that when Jesus was praying "his countenance was altered, and his raiment *became* white *and* dazzling." After Moses had been praying on the mountain his face shone so brightly that the people could not look on it, and he had to wear a veil.

Thus prayer is obviously dynamic and actuates the spiritual ethers that interpenetrate all substance. Prayer is related directly to the creative laws of God, and when man adjusts his mind and body in harmony with those laws, his prayers will always be effective and far-reaching. The activity of the mind that is named the understanding is essential in righteous prayer. Spirit is omnipresent, but the individual consciousness gives it a local habitation and a name.

If in thinking about God we locate Him in a faraway heaven and direct our thoughts outward in the hope of reaching Him, all our force will be driven from us to that imaginary place and we shall become devitalized.

"The kingdom of God is within you." The

pivotal point around which Spirit creates is within the structure of consciousness. This is true of the primal cell as well as of the most complex organ. The throne on which the divine will sits is within man's consciousness, and it is to this inner center that he should direct his attention when praying or meditating. David called this spiritual center of the soul "the secret place of the Most High," and all the defense and power of the 91st Psalm is promised to the one who dwells in the consciousness of the Almighty within. Paul says, "Know ye not that ye are a temple of God, and *that* the Spirit of God dwelleth in you?"

In the 6th chapter of Matthew, in giving His disciples directions for prayer, Jesus called attention to the God center in man in these words: "But thou, when thou prayest, enter into thine inner chamber, and having shut the door, pray to thy Father who is in secret, and thy Father who seeth in secret shall recompense thee." He also told them not to use vain repetitions: "For your Father knoweth what things ye have need of, before ye ask him."

If Divine Mind knows our needs, why should we have to ask to have them supplied? We do not ask expecting God to hand us the things we want, but we realize that He has made provision in the very nature of things for our every need to be fulfilled. When we realize this and go about our work in perfect confidence, the fulfillment of the divine law of support and supply is often demonstrated in ways we had not dreamed of.

Do not supplicate or beg God to give you what

you need, but get still and think about the inexhaustible resources of infinite Mind, its presence in all its fullness, and its constant readiness to manifest itself when its laws are complied with. This is what Jesus meant when He said, "Seek ye first his kingdom, and his righteousness; and all these things shall be added unto you."

We all need a better understanding of the nature of God if we are to comply with the laws under which He creates. We must begin by knowing that "God is Spirit." Spirit is not located in a big man called God but is everywhere the breath of life and the knowing quality of mind active in and through all bodies, "over all, and through all, and in all." The highest form of prayer is to open our minds and quietly realize that the one omnipresent intelligence knows our thoughts and instantly answers, even before we have audibly expressed our desires.

This being true, we should ask and at the same time give thanks that we have already received. Jesus expressed this idea in Mark 11:24: "Therefore I say unto you, All things whatsoever ye pray and ask for, believe that ye receive them, and ye shall have them." Before He broke the miraculously multiplied loaves and fishes and fed the five thousand He looked up to heaven and gave thanks. When He raised Lazarus He first said: "Father, I thank thee that thou heardest me. And I knew that thou hearest me always." Then He commanded Lazarus to come forth.

We observe that all things come out of the formless, but our knowledge of the formless is so limited that we do not conceive of its infinite possibilities. When we think or silently speak in the all-potential ethers of Spirit, there is always an unfailing effect. "Whatsoever ye have said in the darkness shall be heard in the light; and what ye have spoken in the ear in the inner chambers shall be proclaimed upon the housetops."

Silent prayer is more effective than audible, because by silent prayer the mind comes into closer touch with the creative Spirit. James says, "The prayer of faith shall save him that is sick, and the Lord shall raise him up." Countless thousands are applying this faith prayer today and are being healed as men were in the time of Jesus.

The strange thing is that this very important proof of the Spirit's work in Christian healing should have been neglected for so many hundred years when Jesus gave it as one of the signs of a believer: "These signs shall accompany them that believe; in my name shall they cast out demons; they shall speak with new tongues; they shall take up serpents, and if they drink any deadly thing, it shall in no wise hurt them; they shall lay hands on the sick, and they shall recover."

The history of the Christian church records that during its first three hundred years the followers of Jesus healed the sick by prayer and that healing was gradually dropped as the church became prosperous and worldly. A layman from a rural district was being shown, by a bishop, the riches of a cathedral. The bishop said, "The church can no longer say,

'Silver and gold have I none.' " "No," said the layman. "Neither can it say, 'Take up thy bed, and walk.' "

It is found by those who have faith in the power of God that the prayer for health is the most quickly answered. The reason for this is that the natural laws that create and sustain the body are really divine laws, and when man silently asks for the intervention of God in restoring health, he is calling into action the natural forces of his being. Doctors agree that the object of using their remedies is to quicken the natural functions of the body. But medicine does not appeal to the intelligent principle that directs all the activities of the organism, hence it fails to give permanent healing.

However a conscious union with the natural life forces lying within and back of all the complex activities of man gets right to the fountainhead, and the results are unfailing if the proper connection has been made.

The first step in prayer for health is to get still. "Be still, and know that I am God." To get still the body must be relaxed and the mind quieted. Center the attention within. There is a quiet place within us all, and by silently saying over and over, "Peace, be still," we shall enter that quiet place and a great stillness will pervade our whole being. Jesus Christ said, "Peace be unto you. . . . Receive ye the Holy Spirit." That is, He spoke to the within. He said also, "whatsoever ye shall ask in my name, that will I do, that the Father may be glorified in the Son."

"For my thoughts are not your thoughts, neither are your ways my ways, saith Jehovah. For as the heavens are higher than the earth, so are my ways higher than your ways, and my thoughts than your thoughts." This verse from Isaiah gives us an insight into the difference between the mortal thinker and the divine. Divine Mind is serene, orderly, placid, while sense mind is turbulent, discordant, and violent. We can readily understand from this comparison why we do not get divine guidance even though we strive ever so hard for it. The best of us are subject to crosscurrents of worry that interfere with the even flow of God's thoughts into our consciousness. Jesus warned His followers not to be anxious about what they should eat, drink, or wear. In all literature there is no finer comparison than that given by Jesus when He pointed to the flowers and said: "Consider the lilies of the field, how they grow; they toil not, neither do they spin; yet I say unto you, that even Solomon in all his glory was not arrayed like one of these."

If God so clothes the lilies, shall He not much more clothe His children? This argument holds good with reference to all human needs. There is a natural law whose chief purpose is to take care of the human family. But the divine order of creative Mind must be observed by man before he can receive the benefits of his natural inheritance.

Metaphysicians, who study the mind and its many modes of action, find that when they refuse to let thoughts of worry, anxiety, or other distraction act in their minds, they gradually establish an inner quietness that finally merges into a great peace. This is the "peace of God, which passeth all understanding." When this peace is attained, the individual gets inspirations and revelations direct from infinite Mind.

Any method that will hush the external thought clamor will achieve unity with the inner peace. When we are in peaceful sleep, the outer clamor of thought is stilled and the great Spirit of the universe communicates its higher vision to the inner consciousness of man.

The ancient peoples seem to have been more open than moderns to revelations in sleep. Long ago Job wrote in the 33d chapter of his book:

> "In a dream, in a vision of the night,
> When deep sleep falleth upon men,
> In slumberings upon the bed;
> Then he openeth the ears of men,
> And sealeth their instruction."

It is written in I Kings, chapter 3, that the Lord appeared to Solomon in a dream and said, "Ask what I shall give thee." Solomon did not ask for riches, for honor, or for the glory that kings usually seek, but in meekness he asked the Lord to give him an "understanding heart" so that he might discriminate between good and evil and be a wise judge of his people. Riches and honor followed of course, as they always do when a man is earnestly striving to be honest and just in all ways.

We get our most vivid revelations when in a meditative state of mind. This proves that when we make the mind trustful and confident, we put it in harmony with creative Mind; then its force flows to us in accordance with the law of like attracting like.

The agonizing, supplicating, begging prayer is not answered, because the thoughts are so turbulent that Divine Mind cannot reach the pleader. Jesus prayed with a confident assurance that what He wanted would be granted, and He established a mode of prayer for His followers that never fails when the same conditions and relations are attained and maintained with reference to the Father-Mind.

Through His spiritual attainments Jesus formed a spiritual zone in the earth's mental atmosphere; His followers make connection with that zone when they pray in His "name." He stated this fact in John 14:2: "I go to prepare a place for you." Simon Peter said, "Lord, whither goest thou?" Jesus answered him, "Whither I go, thou canst not follow me now; but thou shalt follow afterwards."

When Jesus had purified His body sufficiently, He ascended into this "place" in the spiritual ethers of our planet. In our high spiritual realizations we make temporary contact with Him and His spiritual character, represented by His "name." But we, like the apostles, are not yet able to go there and abide, because we have not overcome earthly attachments. We shall however attain the same freedom and spiritual power that He attained if we follow Him in the regeneration. But we should clearly understand that we cannot go to Jesus' "place" through death. We must overcome death as He did before we can be glorified with Him in the "heavens," the higher realms of the mind.

We should not cease to pray to the Father in the name of Christ Jesus; He said that man should "pray always." Prayer lifts our thoughts on high and sets us free from the narrow limits of matter, just as the electromagnetic impulse is lifted and carried by the ether and caught by any receptive station. Spiritual-minded people are being united today, as in the past, by zones of spiritual force that will eventually become the permanent thought atmosphere of the planet. In Revelation this is typified as the New Jerusalem descending out of the heavens into the earth.

Jesus said we could ask whatsoever we wished in His name and it should be done unto us: "Verily, verily, I say unto you, If ye shall ask anything of the Father, he will give it you in my name. Hitherto have ye asked nothing in my name: ask, and ye shall receive, that your joy may be made full."

Jesus taught in parables because the people did not understand that spiritual forces, acting through mind, make race conditions. But He told them: "The hour cometh, when I shall no more speak unto you in dark sayings, but shall tell you plainly of the Father."

The time prophesied by Jesus—when we should plainly understand the character of the Father—is now at hand, and it behooves all Christians to come out of parables and to realize that scientific laws govern the material, mental, and spiritual realms of Being.

"Pray without ceasing; in everything give thanks," wrote Paul to the Thessalonians. The idea is that we should be persistent in prayer. We know it is always the will of the air to give us all that we can breathe into our lungs. Jesus compared the Spirit to the air in describing the new birth to Nicodemus. It requires lung capacity to breathe deeply of the oceans of air; so it requires spiritual capacity to realize how accessible and ready omnipresent Spirit is to fill us full of itself. The lack is in us. God is more willing to give than we are to receive.

To acquire the mind that is always open to Spirit we must be persistent in prayer. It is written in the 18th chapter of Luke: "And he spake a parable unto them to the end that they ought always to pray, and not to faint." He then told of the judge who feared not God nor man yet who was worn out by the persistency of a woman who demanded justice.

By experimentation modern metaphysical healers have discovered a large number of laws that rule in the realm of mind, and they all agree that no two cases are exactly alike. Therefore one who prays for the health of another should understand that it is not the fault of the healing principle that his patient is not instantly restored. The fault may be in his own lack of persistency or understanding; or it may be due to the patient's dogged clinging to discordant thoughts. In any case the one who prays must persist in this prayer until the walls of resistance are broken down and the healing currents are tuned in. Metaphysicians often pray over a critical case all night,

as history says Luther prayed for the dying Melanchthon and brought about his recovery.

Persistency in prayer awakens the spiritual consciousness and sets into perpetual glow the core of
the soul. When this has been accomplished, one is
in a constant state of thanksgiving and praising, and
the joy of a conscious union with creative Mind is
realized.

CHAPTER VI

God Said, and It Was So

→》》→》》《《←《《←

E MERSON said that the utterance of true ideas by one with a mission causes kings to totter on their thrones. Words of Truth from a zealous man possess dynamic power to heal and bless because the spiritual man enters into them. This is why they move multitudes and are not stayed by conditions or time. When the zone of Spirit, from which healing words emanate, is unobstructed, they feed the souls of men and are creative as well as re-creative. This is why the sayings of the prophets and mystics have such enduring qualities. They are attached by invisible currents of life to the one Great Spirit, and they have within them the germ of perfect wholeness that keeps them perpetually increasing.

The scriptures of the different races are examples of the outward expression of this inner germ. The Book of Job is a dateless work that has been preserved through great changes, including the rise and fall of nations. Who wrote it no one knows, but it was not lost with the loss of its custodians. They were wiped out, their lands taken from them, and they are no longer known among the nations of the earth, but the mystic word of Job was not consumed. If they had applied in their own lives the power of the germ word, the fate of these people would have been very different. But the history of the Book of Job is that of nearly all the sacred writings of all peoples. Secular histories and records of the exploits of men and the affairs of nations have disappeared and been forgotten because they told the tale of the passing world of flesh; but the records of those who had to do with the spiritual are preserved, and they are living today as they have lived ever since they were given forth: through the power derived from Spirit. The true prophet of God does not even have to write his words down. He may speak them to the ethers, and through their own inherent power of perpetuation and growth they will find their way into the minds of men to uplift and to heal. Jesus did not write a line except in the sand, yet His words are treasured today as the most precious that we have.

We know by these many examples that the word of Truth has life in it, that it has power to restore and make whole, and that it cannot perish or grow less with the changes that come with the fleeting years. The more spiritual the individual is who gives forth the words the more enduring they are, and the more powerfully the words move men the more surely they awaken them to their divine nature.

The words of Jesus Christ were given to common people—according to the world's standard—by a carpenter in a remote corner of the earth. Yet these words have moved men for more than nineteen hundred years to realize, to dare, and to do as no other words that were ever uttered.

When Jesus said, "The words that I have spoken unto you are spirit, and are life," He was speaking in terms of that inner Word which creates all things. He knew that His words were vivified with a life essence and a moving power that would demonstrate the truth of His statement.

These words have rung through the souls of men and set them afire with God's Spirit throughout the ages. This is because they are spiritual words, words that have within them the seeds of a divine life, of a perfect wholeness. They grow in the minds of all who give them place, just as a beautiful flower or a great tree grows from the seed germ planted in the ground.

Jesus knew that the consciousness of man was submerged in the things of sense, that it could not perceive Truth in the abstract, and that it must, under these conditions, be stirred into activity through some stimulating force dropped into it from without. Hence He sent forth His powerful words of Truth to the thirsty men, and said unto them, "Keep my word."

To "keep" a word is to resolve it in the mind, to go over it in all its aspects, to believe in it as a truth, and to treasure it as a saving, healing balm in time of need.

All peoples have in all ages known about the saving power of words and have used them to the best of their understanding to cast out demons and to heal the sick. The Hebrews bound upon their foreheads and wrists parchments with words of Scripture written upon them. The Hindus, Japanese, Chinese, and nearly all other nations have their various methods for applying sacred words to the alleviation of their ills, and for invoking the invisible powers to aid them in both their material and their spiritual needs. Although these methods are faulty in that they tend to use the letter of the word instead of its spirit, they are significant as indicators of the universal belief in the power of the sacred word.

We know that words express ideas, and to get at their substantial part we must move into the realm of ideas. Ideas are in the mind, and it is there we must go if we want to get the force of our words. The Hebrew's phylacteries and the Buddhist's prayer wheels are suggestive of the wordy prayers of the Christian; but this is not keeping the words of Jesus, nor reading the inner substance of the mystical words. This can be done only by those who believe in the omnipresent Spirit of God and in faith keep in mind the words that express His goodness, wisdom, power, and wholeness.

Jesus voiced this nearness of God to man more fully than any of the prophets, and His words are correspondingly vivified with the divine inner fire and life and wholeness. He said that those who keep His words will even escape death, so potent is the energy attached to them. This is a startling promise, but when we understand that it was not the personal man Jesus making it but the Father speaking through Him, then we know that it was not an idle one; for He said, "The word which ye hear is not mine, but the Father's who sent me." This is why these words of Jesus endure and why more and more they are attracting the attention of men as the years go by. That is the reason why Jesus' words heal.

Whoever takes Jesus' words into his mind should first consecrate himself to the Truth that they represent. That Truth is not the formulated doctrine of any church nor the creed of any sect; not even of Christianity. That truth is written in the inner sanctuary of every heart, and all men know it without external formulas. It is the intuitive perception of what is right in the sight of God and man. It is this Truth and justice which every man recognizes as the foundation of true living. Whoever consecrates himself to follow the inner monitor, the Spirit of truth, and lives up to its promptings regardless of social or commercial customs has consecrated himself to do God's will, and he is fitted to take Jesus' words and make them his own. His words are then spirit and life.

It is no idle experiment, this keeping in the mind the words of Jesus. It is a very momentous undertaking, which may mark the most important period in the life of the individual. There must be sincerity and earnestness and right motive, and withal a determination to understand its spiritual import. This requires attention, time, and patience in the application of the mind to solving the deeper meanings of the sayings that we are urged to "keep."

People have a way of dealing with sacred words that is too superficial to bring results. They juggle words. They toss them into the air with the heavenly tone or the oratorical ring and count that a compliance with divine requirements. But this is only another form of the prayer wheel and the phylactery. It is that lip service which Jesus condemned, because the purpose is to be "heard of men."

To keep the words of Jesus means much more than this. It has peculiar significance for the inner life, and it is only after this inner life is awakened that the true sense of the spiritual word is understood. But through his devotions the sincere keeper of Jesus' sayings will awaken this inner life or Spirit, and the Lord will come to him and minister to him as carefully as to the adept mystic.

Jesus said, "The words that I have spoken unto you are spirit, and are life." Spirit is that indescribable invisible cause that produces all reality. He who lives in the consciousness of effects alone can know nothing about Spirit, because he has not made himself acquainted with the realm in which it operates. But no one is barred from becoming acquainted with Spirit and residing in its domain. It is just as accessible as the material and far more attractive. If you want to know about Spirit, you will have to take up spiritual ways. You cannot go to the realm of Spirit by traveling the lower road. The road to the realm of Spirit does not lie on the map of the earth, and no man has found it in his physical geography. That spiritual things "are spiritually discerned" was the discovery of someone long ago, but he had no copyright on it. To him it was a revelation, just as it

will be to you and to everyone when it dawns on
the consciousness. It is a great advantage to the spiritual seeker to make this discovery. Millions of persons in every age have tried to find Spirit through
matter and material ways, but they have returned
unsuccessful to the dust. "For verily I say unto you,
that many prophets and righteous men desired to
see the things which ye see, and saw them not; and
to hear the things which ye hear, and heard them
not." They did not fulfill the promise of Jesus, because they saw death and succumbed to its dissolving
hand. They missed the goal because they did not
keep the words of Jesus. They kept the letter instead
of the spirit. They applied in an abstract way what
was intended for everyday practical use.

Jesus tells us that His words are spirit, and then
says to keep them. How can we keep a thing that
we know nothing about? How can we keep the words
and sayings of Jesus unless we get right where He
was and grasp them with our minds?

Surely there is no other way to keep His words.
Those who are trying to do so from any other standpoint are missing the mark. They may be honest and
they may be good, sincere people, living what the
world calls a pure Christian life, but they are not
going to get the fruits of Jesus' words unless they
comply with the requirements.

"There's no getting blood out of a turnip" is a
trite saying. Neither can you get Spirit and life out
of matter and death. Unless you perceive that there
is something more in the doctrine of Jesus than keep-

ing up a worldly moral standard as preparation for
salvation after death, you will fall far short of being
a real Christian.

Jesus did not depreciate moral living; neither
did He promise that it would fulfill the law of God.
Very negative persons are frequently trustworthy
and moral. But that does not make them Christians
after the Jesus Christ plan. Jesus' Christianity had a
living God in it, a God that lived in Him and spoke
through Him. It was a religion of fire and water, of
life as well as purity. Men are to be alive: not merely
exist in a half-dead way for a few years and then go
out with a splutter like a tallow dip. Jesus Christ's
men are to be electric lights that glow and gleam
with perpetual current from the one omnipresent
energy. The connection with that current is to be
made through the mind by setting up sympathetic
energies.

The mind reacts to ideas, and ideas are made
visible in words. Hence the holding of right words
in the mind will set the mind going at a rate propor-
tioned to the dynamic power of the idea back of
the words. A word with a lazy idea back of it will
not stimulate the mind or heal the body. The words
must represent swift, strong spiritual ideas if they
are to infuse the white energy of God into the mind.
This is the kind of words that Jesus reveled in. He
delighted in making great and mighty claims for
His God, for Himself, for His words, and for all
men: "I and the Father are one." "All authority hath
been given unto me in heaven and on earth." "My

Father . . . is greater than all." "Is it not written in your law, I said, ye are gods?" "He that believeth on me, the works that I do shall he do also; and greater works than these shall he do." These were some of the claims with which He stimulated His mind, and He produced the results: He fulfilled His words. He even raised the dead.

But He did not copyright His words or forbid anyone else to use them. He importuned you and me to keep them as He kept them—right in His heart—to realize that this is no idle repetition of words but the setting up of a living fire in the soul that will never go out. This is what the words of Jesus will do for everybody who keeps them in the inner sanctuary of the mind. They will kindle a fire there that will burn higher and higher until it licks the very canopy of heaven and burns a hole in the blue vault of Truth, revealing the wonders of God to the astonished eyes of man.

Jesus' words are varied, but all are food for the minds of His disciples. None of them is too hard for him who would be a disciple, nor is it too far from his present power of realization. What you now comprehend is not the ultimate of your ability in any direction. Your not consciously feeling that you and the Father are one does not militate against its being true. Men in high states of civilization lived for centuries on this planet without knowing that it was a globe and that just across the seas were other continents inhabited like their own. The race today is in the same position as regards the spiritual world. We look with longing eyes across a sea of doubts, fears, and delusions, trying to catch sight of the "Promised Land," but there seems to be no one to pilot us over. But here comes one who is to us a Columbus and who has given us a ship and compass. He has sailed the sea and found the other shore. He asks us to follow Him, and keep His words. His words are the ship and compass.

In about twenty places in the New Testament Jesus is recorded as saying in substance, "Follow me." When we inquire into Jesus' teaching, it is evident that He meant for us to follow His example of being receptive to God's wisdom, peace, power, and health. For instance, let us consider His healing of the man at the Pool of Bethesda who had been afflicted with an infirmity for thirty-eight years.

Now there is in Jerusalem by the sheep *gate* a pool, which is called in Hebrew Bethesda, having five porches. In these lay a multitude of them that were sick, blind, halt, withered. And a certain man was there, who had been thirty and eight years in his infirmity. When Jesus saw him lying, and knew that he had been now a long time *in that case,* he saith unto him, Wouldest thou be made whole? The sick man answered him, Sir, I have no man, when the water is troubled, to put me into the pool; but while I am coming, another steppeth down before me. Jesus saith unto him, Arise, take up thy bed, and walk. And straightway the man was made whole, and took up his bed and walked.

This healing of the man at the pool represents the power of the Christ (typified by Jesus) to restore the equilibrium of the organism through the activity of spiritual ideas in consciousness, independently of the healing methods utilized by the sense man. The true spiritual healing method employs the word of authority, as spoken by Jesus, which must be set into activity. Through the power of the word the "infirmity" gives place to perfect equalization and strength.

To the rich young man who desired to enter into eternal life Jesus recommended the keeping of the commandments, but in addition there was the inevitable "Sell that which thou hast, and give to the poor . . . and come, follow me." Faithfulness to law alone will never make you a follower of Jesus in the regeneration. You must go deeper than this; you must know the inner secrets of the universe. These are revealed in Spirit, and Spirit is found only by those who go about looking for it in an orderly way. People who have for years been students of the science of Christ and who have a clear intellectual perception of its truths are yet outside the kingdom of Spirit. They anxiously ask, "Why is it that I do not realize the presence of Spirit?"

Have you kept the "words" of Jesus? Have you said to yourself in silence and aloud until the very ethers vibrated with its truth, *"I and the Father are one"?* Have you opened your mind by mentally repeating the one solvent of crystallized conditions, "Even as thou, Father, *art* in me, and I in thee"? This means mental discipline day after day and night after night until the inertia of the mind is overcome and the way opened for the descent of Spirit.

The personal consciousness is like a house with all the doors and windows barred. He who lives within may hear voices without, but the doors and windows unlock from within, and it is left to him to unfasten them. The doors and windows of the mind are solidified thoughts, and they swing loose when the right word is spoken to them. Jesus voiced a whole army of right words, and if you will take up His words and make them yours, they will open all the doors of your mind, the light and air will come in, and in due time you will be able to step forth.

No one can do this for you. You do not really want another to do it although you sometimes think how nice it would be if some master of spiritual ideas would suddenly help you right into his understanding. But this is a childish dream of the moment. You want to be yourself, and you can be yourself only by living out your own life and finding its issues at the Fountainhead. If it were possible for one person to reveal the Truth to another, we should have heaven cornered by cunning manipulators of mind and its glories stored up in warehouses awaiting a higher market. Let us be thankful that God is no respecter of persons; that Truth cannot be revealed by one mortal to another. God is a special, personal Father to every one of His children, and from no other source can we get Truth.

Jesus, who has clearly revealed the Father in His consciousness, tells all men how it came about. He points out the way. He says, "I am the way, and the

truth, and the life"; but there is always a condition
attached to its realization by the seeker. He must "believe," he must "keep my words," "follow me."
Summed up, the condition is that by adopting Jesus'
methods you will find the same place in the Father
that He found. But the Father is Spirit and spiritual
understanding is the open sesame to His kingdom.
The secrets of Jesus' words may be said to be in
sealed packages to be opened by those only to whom
is given "the mystery of the kingdom of God."

But Jesus did not peddle His doctrine. He did
not copyright His "words." He claimed to hold con-
verse with the Father, and He demonstrated extraordinary abilities in many ways in substantiation of this
claim. He did not found a sect or in any way fence off
His doctrine. He opened wide the way: "Whosoever
believeth on me" and "keepeth" My words—shall
do thus and so; shall do as I do and do greater
things. He made a special prayer to the Father that
all who kept His word might be made one with the
Father as He was one with Him.

The mighty "words" of Jesus are handed down
to us. By using them in the silent corridors of our
own consciousness we may come into the place
where He now is.

CHAPTER VII

Indispensable Assurance

→>>→>> <<<-<<<-

MAN CAN *be* what he determines to be. He can be master or he can be serf. It rests with him whether he shall fill the high places in life or the low, whether he shall serve or be served, lead or be led, or be sickly or healthy. Of course we understand that these distinctions are relative only; in the sight of the Most High the servant may be prized more than his master, but there is within every one an inherent desire to be at the top, which desire has its root deep down in our very nature and is consequently legitimate. That it is frequently misdirected and used toward base ends is no reason why it should be depreciated. We all desire to excel. This desire is the inspiration of Spirit, which ever forces us up through earth toward heaven, and it should be encouraged and cultivated in the right direction.

A man without ambition is like a ship afloat on the waves without sails or power. Such a man simply drifts: if he reaches port safely it is by chance.

But a ship under full sail or power needs one other important thing and that is a rudder. Then it needs a man to handle that rudder, and that man needs faith.

In considering the character of faith we must start, as we do with everything else, in the one Mind.

God must have had faith in order to ideate the universe before it was created; and man, being like God, must base his creations on faith. Faith is innate in man. A favorite definition of faith is that of Paul: "Faith is the assurance of things hoped for, a conviction of things not seen." It is by works of faith that we develop our consciousness and heal ourselves. The important question with everyone of us is, How does faith work?

It is possible to have a reality and yet neither touch it nor smell it nor see it nor in any way come into consciousness of it in the outer realm. That is what faith is. It is the consciousness in us of the realities of the attributes of mind. Before we can have the substance of faith we must realize that the mind creates realities. How do we create realities without seeing them, or feeling them, or smelling them, or tasting them, or in any way coming into outer consciousness of them? Faith is the wonderful power that builds these eternally real things.

Faith is a power of the spiritual mind, but in all the realms of existence we find faith. The foundation of faith is in the spiritual, but wherever you find the mind at work you find faith. Faith in its highest form is an exalted idea. And what is the most exalted idea that man can have? That he is spiritual; that he is related directly to the one great Spirit, and that through that Spirit he can do mighty works by faith.

Jesus laid great stress on faith. He always tried to direct the attention of the people to the invisible, the spiritual, by statements like these: "Believe ye that I am able to do this?" "According to your faith be it done unto you." "Thy faith hath made thee whole." All through His works there runs a golden thread of faith. Jesus did not advocate faith in material forces of any character. Through faith He healed thousands. His command was "Have faith in God."

We would not destroy anyone's faith in the lesser things, but would give him a sure foundation for all faith by directing his attention to the one and only source of faith, Divine Mind. The question for us is how to increase our faith in Spirit. You will find that you have plenty of faith. All men have faith, but it is scattered here and there and everywhere by being placed in lesser things, and those lesser things finally fail us.

If you get a good strong perception of something that your inner mind tells you is true, act upon it, and you will find that it will come true.

In developing His apostles Jesus took Peter as the representative of faith, and proclaimed that upon this foundation (of faith) He would build the new man, His "church" or aggregation of spiritual ideas. The faith demonstrated by Peter in the beginning of his career was not of a very high type. When Truth (represented by Christ) was being tried, Peter denied Jesus: said that he did not know Him and swore at Him, showing that Peter's faith must have been at a very low ebb when put to the test. At the very last Jesus tried Peter again and again, asking three times, "Lovest thou me?" Faith and love are very closely related. You must love the Lord, and then you must have faith in His spiritual power and continuity. Peter finally unfolded a mighty healing power. Even his shadow healed.

Now this faith that we are all cultivating and striving for is built up through continuous affirmations of its loyalty to the divine idea, the higher self. You must have faith in your spiritual capacity.

Many have learned how to hold the truth about health steadily in faith even in the midst of the most adverse appearances, and they clearly understand that they are not telling falsehoods when they deny sickness right in the face of the appearance of it. In the same way we achieve our victory over sin. When ill temper, vanity, greed, selfishness, and other sins of greater and lesser degree come up, they should be denied; and the unselfishness, the purity, the uprightness, and the integrity of the higher self should be affirmed. Persons who are quickened spiritually can do very much greater works through the law of faith than those who are still in the material consciousness; and once having discerned the power of Spirit, we should be on our guard and send forth on every occasion exalted ideas of the spiritual.

"I am the living bread which came down out of heaven: if any man eat of this bread, he shall live for ever." Jesus Christ raised people who had let go of the life idea and brought them into such a consciousness of omnipresent life that they came out of the tomb.

This life consciousness that Jesus Christ quickens is as greatly needed in our day as it was in the time when He first worked in the souls of men. If you go to a medical doctor and ask him the cause of your ills, he will tell you that most of them come from lack of vitality, which means lack of life. We all need vitalizing. The question is, How shall we get life? What is the source of life? Those who teach the use of material remedies point us to various things as the source—food, air, water, and so forth; but those who depend on these remedies are fast losing faith in drugs and are reaching out to electricity and similar means of gaining more abundant life. They are thus getting a little closer to the healing system of Jesus, but they still lack the all-important truth that God is life and that they who worship Him must worship Him in the life consciousness, that is, in Spirit. When we worship God in His way, we are vitalized all at once; there is no other way to get real, permanent life. We cannot get life from the outer man or from anything external; we must touch the inner current.

The life source is spiritual energy. It is deeper and finer than electricity or human magnetism. It is composed of ideas, and man can turn on its current by making mental contact with it.

When Jesus came teaching the gospel of Spirit, people did not understand Him. They did not know that universal Spirit is Principle and that we demonstrate it or fail to demonstrate it according to the character of our thinking. It has taken the race two thousand years to find that we turn on the life current by means of thoughts and words. We can have fullness of life by realizing that we live in a sea of abundant, omnipresent, eternal life, and by refusing to allow any thought to come in that stops the consciousness of the universal life flow. We live and move and have our being in life, Mind life. You can think of your life as mental; every faculty will begin to buzz with new life. Your life will never wane if you keep in the consciousness of it as Mind or Spirit; it will increase and attain full expression in your body. If you have faith in the life idea in your consciousness, your body will never be run down but will become more and more alive with spiritual life until it shows forth the glory of Christ.

We must think life, talk life, and see ourselves filled with the fullness of life. When we are not manifesting life as we desire, it is because our thoughts and our conversation are not in accord with the life idea. Every time we think life, speak life, rejoice in life, we are setting free, and bringing into expression in ourselves more and more of the life idea. Here is the place of abundant life, and we can fill both mind and body, both our surroundings and our affairs, with glad, free, buoyant life by exercising faith in it. "According to your faith be it done unto you."

In this way we enter into the same consciousness of abundant, enduring, unfailing, eternal life that Jesus had, and we can readily understand His proclamation that those who believe in the indwelling

Christ life will never die. If we are wise, we shall cultivate faith in and understanding of omnipresent life.

I know a man who is a natural pessimist, and if anyone mentions something that is not to be emulated he will say, "Now, let us be careful about that." If you speak of someone who has been doing a good work for the community, he will always throw in a little depreciation. His whole life has been like sodden bread. Everything falls flat in his affairs, and he does not understand why it is. He says, "I have been studying this Truth for years, and I do not understand why I do not succeed." Intellectually he is a Truth seeker, but it has not taken hold of his faith substance. He doubts, and down he goes. When Peter tried to walk on the water to meet Jesus, he went down in the sea of doubt. He saw too much wetness in the water. He saw the negative side of the proposition, and it weakened his demonstration. If you want to demonstrate, never consider the negative side. If mountains seem to oppose the carrying out of your plans, say with Napoleon that there shall be no Alps. The man who is grounded in faith does not measure his thoughts or his acts by the world's standard of facts. "Faith is blind," say people who are not acquainted with the real thing; but those who are in spiritual understanding know that faith has open eyes, that certain things do exist in Spirit and become substantial and real to the one who dwells and thinks and lives in faith. Such a one knows.

Many Christians are like the woman who was on a ship during a great storm. She went to the captain and said, "Now I want to know just how bad it is." He told her plainly that they were in a very desperate and helpless condition and finished by saying, "We shall have to trust in God." She exclaimed, "Oh, dear! has it come to that?"

A close analysis shows that faith is the foundation of all that man does. The doctor knows that the patient's faith in him and his method is essential to his success. I remember a story told me by a lawyer: A certain attorney was subject to periodical headaches. He had some capsules prescribed by his physician that would cure these headaches almost instantly. For emergencies he carried one of the capsules in his vest pocket, and immediately upon swallowing it the pain would disappear. Once when pleading a case he was seized with a headache. He reached into his pocket, secured the little antidote and swallowed it, and immediately the headache left him. He went on with his argument, and after he sat down he wished to make some corrections in his notes, and felt in his pocket for a little rubber pencil tip that he carried for that purpose. Instead of the rubber tip he brought out a capsule, thus discovering that he had swallowed his pencil tip instead of the capsule.

This was an exhibition of faith asserting itself unawares. Suppose we should concentrate such faith on the invisible, the real things, the things of Spirit, how wonderful would be our demonstrations! How

effective we should become in using the mighty working power of Spirit!

Jesus told His followers (and we are all His
followers) to go forth and do His works—raise the
dead and the like—and that we should do even
greater works than He did. How? By exercising spiritual faith, by increasing our power through exalted
ideas. We must raise our faith to the very highest
in us and rest in the "assurance" or substance of its
reality.

Jesus had faith in God, and this gave Him faith
in all men. Spiritual understanding reveals the uni-
versality of all things. When they brought to Him
the lame man on the couch, letting him down
through the ceiling, "Jesus seeing their faith," healed
him, not because of the faith of the man himself
but because of the faith of those who brought him.
The faith of his neighbors in the power of Spirit
did the work for the sick man.

We believe that doctors are doing the very best
they know; but if they would only approach a little
closer to the spiritual, what a wonderful work they
might do! They are giving less and less medicine every year. They recognize more and more that there
is something back of medicine that they call the healing power of nature.

Nearly every doctor of large experience will tell
you that he can get the same result with a little
sweetened water that he can with drugs if he has
the confidence of the patient. If the patient can be
made to believe that the drug is going to work in

a certain way, he will carry out this belief to the letter. Thus the word, the imagination, and faith work together.

Jesus had this high spiritual realization, and He healed through the word. He is the Great Physician. He is the one whom we are to follow, whom we are seeking to emulate; and we do it through laying hold of Spirit. I would say to you that if you want to do the works of God, you must follow Christ. If you want to elevate yourself out of the physical, you must have faith in God and must cultivate that faith through affirmation of your spiritual power and faith. The Lord's Prayer is continual affirmation from beginning to end.

It has been our experience in developing the faculties of mind that the more we affirm a certain thing the stronger it becomes. But we must have the understanding that our relation to God is that of a son to his father; that we exist in the one Mind as an idea, and that this idea does work in us as in a superman, even Christ.

It is a metaphysical law that there are three steps in every demonstration; the recognition of Truth as it is in principle; holding the idea; and acknowledging fulfillment. Pray believing that you have received, and you shall receive.

From the teaching of Jesus it is clear that He accepted fully the proposition that God is our resource and that all things are provided for us by our Father. It is necessary to cultivate these ideas by considering them daily in all that we do.

It is recorded that a pupil of Socrates' once said to him: "Master, when we read what you have inscribed we are inspired; when we come into your presence we are moved to love; when we hear your words we are charmed, and when we touch your hand we are thrilled."

Socrates was a great soul, a master mind, and his soul radiation was very powerful. But Jesus was still greater in His soul radiation; He had through ages of discipline and thought projection in word and deed made Himself a master scientist in the mental and spiritual worlds. His soul radiation or aura was so powerful that it perpetually stimulates to greater achievement and thrills with new life all who enter its sphere of influence. Thought transference is an accepted fact to many persons, and it is sustained by the recent tests in measuring the force projected in the process of human thinking. Machines have been invented so sensitive that they respond to the thoughts of men and women under various emotions. The results are reported to be so pronounced in their order and regularity as to constitute a universal law in mind activity.

This power of the mind to project the results of thinking gives us the key to the work of Jesus in resurrecting His body and making it perpetually radiant in our mental and spiritual atmosphere.

As there are dimensions above that in which we live so there are levels of mind activity above and beyond the intellectual. Jesus said, "In my Father's house are many mansions"; that is, dwelling places in mind or consciousness: states of consciousness.

"I go to prepare a place for you. . . . that where I am, *there* ye may be also."

The assertions by physical scientists that we have no assurance of any power that will increase our moral stature or save us from suffering and degeneracy is beyond comprehension to one who has gone deeply into the study of psychology and spiritual dynamics.

We may receive spiritual inspiration from within. By prayer and meditation on words of Truth in the silence we may so open our consciousness to the inner divine presence that the necessary understanding, love, and power may be given us to enable us to bring forth in our own lives the good results that we wish to see manifest. This is much better than waiting to see the demonstrations of others before believing and before attempting to bring forth demonstrations of our own.

After Thomas was shown the evidence he believed. After the outer reason sees the works accomplished by the I AM by means of faith and the word it accepts Truth. But there is a quicker way to grow in faith and in spiritual understanding, a way that has nothing to do with intellectual reasoning and belief. Jesus said, "Blessed *are* they that have not seen, and *yet* have believed." That way is the quickening of our innate spiritual faith.

True faith in God separates itself from all negative belief in the body as material, impure, transient.

With the growth of faith in the mind of the individual there comes a quickening of all his thoughts by the influx of Truth. "The word of God" increases.

God is never absent from you. He is constantly taking form in your life according to the exact pattern of your words, thoughts, and actions. Just as soon as you really bring your words and your expectations up to the measure of God's love for you, just that soon you will demonstrate.

Thoughts are seeds that, when dropped or planted in the subconscious mind, germinate, grow, and bring forth their fruit in due season. The more clearly we understand this truth the greater will be our ability to plant the seeds that bring forth desirable fruits. After sowing the plants must be tended. After using the law we must hold to its fulfillment. This is our part, but God gives the increase. You must work in divine order and not expect the harvest before the soil has been prepared or the seed sown. You have now the fruits of previous sowings. Change your thought seeds and reap what you desire. Some bring forth very quickly, others more slowly, but all in divine order.

The law of spiritual healing involves full receptivity on the part of the one under treatment. God does not do things in us against our will, as will acts in both the conscious and subconscious realms of mind. However much it may appear that the word is thwarted in its original intent, this is never true; it goes on, and it enters where reception is given it. In this way men are quickened, and whether we see the result with our physicial vision or not, the process is as sure as God Himself.

In treating others we are told to see our patients as perfect. So in actualizing our ideals we must see them as if they were part of our phenomenal life. We often hear it said that the genius lives in a world of his own, separate and apart from common minds. From the metaphysical standpoint we see that the genius is merely one who has caught onto the law of believing his dreams of health, perfection, and success to be true, and whose dreams have therefore become true.

A genius is one who lets the full Spirit within him speak out, regardless of how different its utterances may be from those of people who have posed as authority. He has absolute faith in his spiritual revelations and fearlessly proclaims them. He is a pioneer and a leader. He listens to his own inherent genius and has faith in his God-given ability. Not only must he listen but he must act. The world is filled with original dreamers. They have ideas brilliant beyond expression, but they do not clothe them in the habiliments of action.

You must not only perceive and idea; you must also give it form by infusing into it the substance of your living faith. Daydreamers may be found by the score in physics and metaphysics. They all fall short in failing to realize that there are two sides to every proposition, the image and the expression: and that the Lord God formed man out of the ground and breathed into his nostrils the breath of life.

So each one of us must not only see the image

of his desires as a theory, but he must also form it into a living, breathing thing through every motive and act of his life. That is, if we have an idea, we must act just as if it were part of our life. We must be formed from the substance of our world, whether it be the dust of the ground or the ethers of the invisible. There must be an actual imaging of them in our consciousness before we shall ever see our ideas realized.

Here is where the dreamer and the divine scientist part company. One says, "I admire your theories greatly, but they can never be realized on this earth. Things are as they are, and they cannot be changed. We are here, and we shall just have to make the best of it."

He who has learned the meaning of man—who and what man is—never allows himself to make any such admissions. He knows that there is a way provided by which he not only can lift himself out of the swamp of belief in sin, sickness, and death but also through his efforts open the way for many others to find the way to perfection. No man ever demonstrated his God-given powers in even a small way who did not help many others to do likewise. Preaching is good, but practice is better. "I, if I be lifted up from the earth, will draw all men unto myself."

There is a work for everyone who will listen and obey the Spirit. That work is important, because it is eternal and brings results eternal in their nature.

If you have heard the voice of the Lord and are

obedient to it at any cost, you are chosen. Your life is hid with Christ in God, and the way into the kingdom is assured you.

This is no fanciful sketch, nor does it refer to a theoretical place or condition to be reached in some future state or under circumstances more propitious. This kingdom of God is now existing right here in our midst. It is being externalized little by little.

Whoever has a high, pure thought and affirms his allegiance to it as a part of his daily life is adding to the externality of that kingdom among men. Whoever says, *"I will be upright and honest in all that I think and do,"* is laying the foundation stones for one of the buildings of the New Jerusalem.

Whoever affirms his allegiance to the good, regardless of all appearance of evil, and in dealing with his brother declares by word and act that only the good exists, is building white spires to the one and only true God.

Whoever lays up in his mental storehouse the resolve *"I will do unto others as I would have them do unto me"* is paving the highways with pure gold in a heavenly city of equity and justice.

There will be no need of the sun or the moon in the city of the kingdom of God, because God, the good, will be the light thereof.

We are the temples of God, of good, and through us is this light to shine, which is so bright as to dim the rays of those shining orbs of the night and the day. Herein is God glorified that we love one another. Herein does the true light shine that we let love and peace and kindness shine forth forever and always. We are to be the very light itself and we can only be the light by becoming so pure that it cannot help but shine through us. This is possible to the highest and lowest in the world's roster of respectability. We are all the chosen of the Lord and we make the covenant that carries us into His visible presence by laying down the personal man and taking up the universal man. He it is that thunders in the depths of our soul. "Who say ye that I am?"

CHAPTER VIII

The Fullness of Time

->>>->>> <<<-<<<-

ALL SANE persons acknowledge the necessity of observing the laws of health in their daily living, but the great majority have a human standard. Now that the whole race is awakening to the knowledge of a higher source of existence more people every day are giving attention to the law of Spirit in their life.

"Order is heaven's first law." If we desire to demonstrate health when we receive more spiritual life, we must order this life rightly, for if it is not so ordered, mental and physical discord will ensue. This applies to all that we think and do. Everything must be brought into order. If we affirm prosperity, that too must be brought into orderly relations to the rest of our thinking. We may be declaring life and prosperity and at the same time be holding some disorganizing thought. This will produce inharmony and discord in body and affairs. Lack of orderly arrangement of thoughts is responsible for many delayed demonstrations of healing.

We find in the Scriptures constant reference, in symbols and also in direct language, to order as a fundamental law of the universe and of man. There must be order in the spiritual life as well as the material life. All peoples have observed this, and especially the people of God. Paul said, "Let all things be done decently and in order."

Suggestion is systematically used in the business world, and unless you are strong in your own convictions as to what your needs are, you will be loaded up with many things for which you have no use. The remedy is to establish yourself in the spiritual law. You will come under one or the other of these laws, the man-made or the spiritual, and it is for you to choose which is best.

You want to know then the metaphysics of order as a means of demonstrating health. How can you order your life by the divine plan? By accepting it as a truth that there is such a plan and by making this plan yours through affirming your oneness with the omnipresent Mind in which this plan exists in its righteousness. Say, *"I am the offspring of God, and I am one with His perfect wisdom, which is now ordering my life in divine harmony and health."* Ask for wisdom; then affirm divine order. Put yourself in unity with Spirit. Then you will come into the consciousness of a new world of thought and act and find yourself doing many things differently because the orderly Mind that directs the universe is working through you. A harmonious relation will be established in all your ways. Whatever there was in mind, body, or affairs that was out of harmony will easily be adjusted when you open the way in your mind for the manifestation of divine order.

The bringing forth of man even in the material sense is an orderly process. The birth of Jesus is an example. His coming was foretold and arranged beforehand. It was not left to chance. His mother "magnified" the Lord before He was born. This illustrates the truth that it is necessary to have order from the very beginning. The bringing forth of John the Baptist is an example of the coming of another state of consciousness and of the necessity of law and order in prenatal culture.

The same law holds good in our body and our affairs. The power of the word should be expressed in our homes. We should surround ourselves with words suggestive of spiritual things. If words count, and we know they do, we should be careful of every idea taken into consciousness through the eye as well as through the ear.

From their inception to their expression words are important. The law is fulfilled not only in mind but in manifestation also. Every suggestion that enters the mind brings forth like expression in act. The time is coming when it will be unlawful to print in the daily papers any record of crime or of anything that will bring discord into the minds of readers. Recently I read of a man who committed a crime, and in his pocket was found a newspaper clipping describing almost identically the same criminal act. His crime was the fruit of suggestion. How many such suggestions does one large daily paper carry to its thousands of readers in its recital of the daily horrors that make up the news?

As the world comes more and more under the spiritual law editors and publishers will not ask their readers what they want, but will give them what they should have for mental food. And as the people are raised to higher planes of consciousness they will demand reading of an uplifting character. They will be just as careful as regards what they read as they are now beginning to be in reference to food. There will be the same demand for pure reading as for pure food. If it is against the law of the land to adulterate food, how much more is it against the law of right thinking to adulterate the truth. We can see the necessity of order and law according to Spirit. If we would demonstrate health, every deleterious thought should be kept out of our mental atmosphere even more carefully than harmful elements are kept out of our material food.

This spiritual law is operative in food and clothing. If we think about order and harmony our taste in material things will change. We shall desire the purest foods, and there will be more harmony in the colors we choose to wear. "If God doth so clothe the grass of the field . . . *shall he* not much more *clothe* you?" Some people think it is impossible for man to be clothed like the lilies. But if man stands above all creation, has he not power to clothe himself in the richness and glory of Spirit? Out of the air we may manufacture the things we eat and wear. This is not a flight of fancy. Chemists are already considering the possibility. It is not an assumption of theoretical metaphysics that we may be able to make our food and clothing from the air, but a logical conclusion that follows the understanding of God as the omnipresent source of all that appears.

So long as we believe in the slow processes of what we call nature we shall place ourselves under a law of slowness. But if we know the spiritual law of health and the power of the word, we shall bring into operation in our lives an entirely different law. Where is the limit to the power of thought?

So let us begin anew and lay down the law of order in all that we do. If there is a tendency to hurry, let us stop and affirm divine order and rest ourselves in its poise. Geologists tell us that our world has been whirling around the sun for over five hundred million years. So you see there is no need to hurry. Remember that you live in eternity now. This thought of omnipresent eternity will alleviate nervous tension. Put every thought and act under the divine law. Even if you think you are going to miss a car, do not hurry. Another car will be right along, and if your mind is in divine order, it will be your car.

If you are disorderly and indefinite along any line, put yourself at once under the order of Divine Mind by affirming daily that the same law that swings the stars in the cushioned ethers is operative in and through your life and all your affairs.

All people who have studied metaphysics and understand somewhat the action of the mind recognize that there is one underlying law and that through this law all things come into expression; also that there is one universal Mind, the source and sole origin of all real intelligence. First is mind, then mind expresses itself in ideas, then the ideas make themselves manifest. This is a metaphysical statement of the divine Trinity, Father, Son, and Holy Spirit. The trinity Mind, the expression of Mind, and the manifestations of Mind are found in simple numbers and complex combinations everywhere.

The metaphysics of the Hebrew Scriptures are based on this law of the Trinity. They were written far ahead of the race thought, and it is probable that those who wrote them did not understand all that was involved in the word of the Spirit. It is seldom that great writings are fully understood. Not many years after Shakespeare's demise a book aiming to give the names of all the English poets was published in London, and Shakespeare's name was left out. It is said that a great man must be dead five hundred years before his work will be appreciated.

In the King James Bible the Hebrew "Jehovah" has been translated "Lord." Lord means an external ruler. Bible students say that Jehovah means the self-existent One, the I AM. Then instead of reading "Lord" we should read I AM. It makes a great difference whether we think of I AM, self-existence within, or "Lord," master without. All Scripture shows that Jehovah means just what God told Moses it meant: I AM. "This is my name for ever, and this is my memorial unto all generations." So instead of "Lord" say I AM whenever you read it and you will get a clearer understanding and realization of what Jehovah is. God was known to the Israelites as Jehovah-shalom: "I am peace." You can demonstrate peace of mind by holding the words *"I am peace."*

If we start any such demonstration and try to apply the I AM to personality, we fall short. This is frequently the cause of lack of results in carrying out the laws that all metaphysicians recognize as fundamentally true. The mind does not always comprehend the I AM in its highest, neither does it discern that the all-knowing, omnipotent One is within man. This recognition must be cultivated, and everyone should become conscious of the I AM presence. This consciousness will come through prayer and meditation upon Truth. In Truth there is but one I AM, Jehovah, the omnipotent I AM that is eternally whole and perfect. If you take Jehovah-shalom into your mind and hold it with the thought of a mighty peace, you will feel a consciousness, a harmonizing stillness, that no man can understand. This consciousness is healing in itself. It must be felt, realized, and acknowledged by your individual I AM before the supreme I AM can pour out its power. Then you will know that you have touched something; but you cannot explain to another just what it is, because you have gone beyond the realm of words and made union with the divine cause. It is the quickening of your divinity through the power of the word. This divine nature is in us all, waiting to be brought into expression through our recognition of the power and might of the I AM; so Jehovah-rapha is "I am he that healeth thee."

We should not fail to think always of the spiritual law under which the I AM moves. It is possible for man to take I AM power and apply it in external ways and leave out the true spiritual law. In our day we are proclaiming that man can use I AM power to restore health and bring increased happiness; in fact, that through righteous, lawful use of the I AM he can have everything that he desires. But some people are using this power in a material way, neglecting soul culture, building up the external without taking the intermediate step between the supreme Mind and its manifestation in the outer. We should remember that the soul must grow as well as the body. For example, a man was overtaken with physical disability and loss of eyesight some years ago. In his extremity he turned to the spiritual law for help and was very faithful in its mental application. I saw him not long since; his physical condition was unchanged, but there was a great change in his mind. He had found the light and he was filled with inward rejoicing. He had become blind that he might see. However his family thought all his dependence upon Truth had been a failure because his physical sight had not been restored. During all these years however he has managed his business, and it has prospered, and his family has been well provided for. He was himself for a time disappointed and rebellious because his eyes were not healed; but now he is glad, because through the prayers and meditations he has found the inner light. His physical sight will be restored when he has made the complete connection between mind and body.

So if you find yourself disappointed because you do not at once demonstrate health or success, be at peace and know that your earnest prayers and meditations are working out in you a soul growth that will yet become manifest beyond your greatest hopes.

It is easier to seek the Truth willingly and be watchful and obedient than it is to be forced by some severe experience. Hard experiences are not necessary if we are obedient to the Truth that saves us from them. Time should be given to prayer and meditation daily. We cannot grow without them, and no man who neglects them will successfully develop his spiritual powers.

The great I AM is not far away from man. Spirit is closely connected with the little things of daily life. "The kingdom of God is come nigh unto you." This means that the mighty One is with us in all ways. We are all in touch, heart with heart, and a real sympathy makes us one. In reality we all love the simple life. The pomp and parade and pageantry of the external world do not satisfy the soul. It is the small things that touch the heart and appeal to us. We want realities. Even in the drama we demand the realistic. I once read of a playwright who tried to give all his scenes the touch of realism, and in one place he had electric fans so placed that they would blow to the audience the odors of the viands that the actors were eating, thus convincing the people that the food was real.

While one of his plays was being given a cat strayed in, stretched before the fireplace, lay down and went to sleep. The audience applauded. This added a touch of naturalness that the playwright

was anxious to introduce as a permanent feature of
the play. But it is hard to get a cat to do things when
you want it to do them. However the playwright set
himself to studying how he could induce the cat to
go through with its part, and he hit upon this plan:
About noon each day he shut the cat up in a very
small box so that it had no room to stretch; then he
let it out just at the time its appearance on the stage
was desired. Of course the first thing it did was to
stretch, then drink from a saucer of milk set ready
for it; then it would lie down before the fireplace
and go to sleep. So he solved the problem, and this
little touch of commonplace realism became the hit
of the play.

It is on such little things as these that success
hinges in the play called "life." The I AM might is
not in the storm nor in the earthquake nor in the
fire but in the "still small voice," according to Elijah.

We are receiving new truth in all fields, and
if we are to use it, it seems most important that our
religion be progressive, that we get new and higher
concepts, and that we see deeper and more scientific
relations in the lessons and experiences of those who
have preceded us in study and demonstration of spiritual Truth.

If there is science in the universe, there must be
science in the Mind that projected the universe. If
there is mathematical accuracy and order in the material world, there is a like accuracy and order in
the mental world. If there is science in the relation
of atom to atom, if there is science in the current

that flows over the wire and sets in motion the electric fan, there must be science in the Mind back of all these manifestations.

God created all things by His mind, by His thought, by the power of His word. The divine fiat went forth, "Let there be," and there was. The one Mind is still projecting itself into the universe, and its law of health is expressed by man through thought rightly directed. The highest expression of divine thought is man. God created man in His image, in the image of perfect health. How important then that man should study the science of mind and in every way seek to find the law lying back of the harmonious universe in which he functions.

If we make living cells through the power of thought, we should know something of the law underlying the process. On every hand thoughtful men are searching for the scientific cause of things. Here is an illustration that came to my attention. The woman in the case, an ardent Unity student, had a husband who thought Truth was all foolishness. She did not urge it upon him directly, but she would call his attention to various healings. He paid no attention until his mother was healed of a mole on her face. This woman said to her husband: "Your mother's healing was due to the withdrawal of her nourishing thought. That mole is gone." "How did it go?" he asked, showing some interest for the first time. His mother said: "I withdrew the nourishing thought. Before that I had mourned over it and wished it were not there, and that nourished it and sent vital forces into it and it kept growing." "I suggested that she quit thinking about it," said the wife; "that she quit nourishing it, and it gradually withered and disappeared." The husband said: "I can see how through our thought we do nourish these conditions in our bodies. If there is such power behind this healing system I am willing to think about it. There is something satisfactory in knowing that one may learn how healing works. I can see as a reasonable proposition that mind acts on the body through nerves and that the conditions are nourished by thought. When Mother stopped thinking about that mole, it was no longer nourished and consequently disappeared. That appeals to my reason. I thought this was a religion, a sect; but if it is something that a logical mind can understand, I want to know more about it." You will find persons like that everywhere. They think this is some new religion, and when they come to understand that it is absolute science they are willing to look into it. This man saw the truth when it was explained to him.

We may nourish a good thing by thinking how good it is—a beautiful face, a beautiful form, whatever it may be that is good; but suppose we take the negative side, shall we then get results also? Yes, absolutely. We shall get just what we think about. The thought of nourishing is a very good thought, because it shows us just what we do. Our mind draws upon the vital forces, and according to physiological laws we alter our tissues. Either we tear down our bodies or we build them up.

Is that all that is necessary? No, that is only one phase of mind activity. Withdraw the error; then build in the good. Some people leave out this second step. When you get into this understanding of the mind it is always good to use both the denial and the affirmation. Sometimes the denial will produce wonderful results. But this law of the mind working on the body is applicable to both the inner and the outer.

You will get suggestions from newspapers. You may read about some healing drug and a description of how your cold is going to develop into pneumonia and then into consumption if you do not buy some of it. You read the advertisement, which describes in minute detail how terrible you feel, and you say, "Yes, that's my case exactly." If you do this, you will nourish that sick thought. Is it wise then to let this law of mind operate in this way? No. Avoid these things. Don't give yourself up to them.

The universe was not created through illogical assumptions of law. Law is its foundation. There are no miracles in science. Jesus did no miracles. All His marvelous works were done under laws that we may learn and use as He did. As the body is moved by mind, so the mind is moved by ideas; and right here in the mind we find the secret of the universe. This is where Jesus differed from ordinary men: He knew He was the Son of God; He knew the power of spiritual ideas to do mighty works: "The Father abiding in me doeth his works."

Before you can realize the mighty power of
ideas you must unify them. All must pull together.
Get your ideas in divine order, and a mighty mind
force will begin to work for you right away. This
divine order is necessary to the upbuilding of both
mind and body. This divine order is the "kingdom
of heaven" so often referred to by Jesus. To attain
this unity and harmony of mind it is necessary to
have perfect statements of Truth and to adhere to
them in thought and word. States of mind can be
set into activity just as through the manipulation of
gases, electricity, and so forth we may purify or im-
part certain potencies to the atmosphere. In a far
larger degree ideas change the race thought atmosphere. Jesus had a grasp of divine ideas, and if
we believe in and follow Him we shall come into
the Christ state of mind. We become like-minded by
entering into the absolute Mind. In the absolute
Mind there is only harmony.

Spirit is a vigorous stimulant. It uplifts the whole
consciousness, vitalizes the organs, and gives us
courage and endurance. It also tends to make one
supersensitive. In this state one is liable to more
rapid waste, especially if fleshly indulgence of any
kind is gratified. Failing to restrain one's passions
and appetites quickly burns up the cells, and then the
collapse is even more complete than before the healing. In order to guard against this students should
be instructed carefully in the truths of Being. They
must learn that "the wages of sin is death," that they
must master their appetites and passions.

As man unifies his own mind forces in the one Mind his body is lifted up into a new state of harmony. If he is not demonstrating this principle, it is because he is not unified with the one great harmonious Mind. He is not expressing this Mind as he should because he is not realizing his oneness with it. Resolve to become one with God through Christ. Harmonize yourself with Him and all your world will be in harmony. Be on the alert to see harmony everywhere. Do not magnify seeming differences. Do not keep up any petty divisions but continually declare the one universal harmony. This will insure perfect order and wholeness. The Christ Mind is here as the unifying principle of this race, and we must believe in this mind working in us and through us and know that through it we are joined to the Father-Mind. That is the Father's house to which, like the prodigal son, we have all so long been seeking to return. In the consciousness of the Father-Mind the unity of God and man is demonstrated.

The fact that you can always return to the Father's house, the ideal world, carries with it the possibility of fulfillment in your life expression. In Being you cannot shirk expression. To think is to express, and you are doing that without cessation. You may deny that these things of the world have existence, yet so long as you live in contact with them you are recognizing their place. A wholesale denial of their existence keeps you even as a house divided against itself. A reconciliation must take place before you can demonstrate the power of the Christ man over death. Jesus did not say that His body was nothing, but He did say, "I have power to lay it down, and I have power to take it again." He laid it down in corruption and raised it up in incorruption. He found that His ideal was not being expressed in the body, which was subject to decay; so He let the corruptible be crossed out and from the ruins raised the body of light, which appeared and disappeared at will. This was the fulfillment of His ministry and the demonstration of the power of the Spirit to overcome the last enemy, death.

All men desire to overcome disease and death. The fulfillment of this desire would be the perpetuation of existence in form. So in the last analysis we see that we all want to continue our chain of expression indefinitely, without break. This has always been the desire of mankind, and the whole world is today and ever has been fighting this monster death. Oceans of medicine are swallowed daily, millions of doctors are exerting all their energies, and prayers unnumbered are uttered in a blind struggle to vanquish this dreaded enemy of mankind. This indicates a most powerful desire to be fulfilled. Jesus showed how it might be done and gave the recipe. He said, "Verily, verily, I say unto you, If a man keep my word, he shall never see death." He also said: "The word which ye hear is not mine, but the Father's who sent me" and "The words that I have spoken unto you are spirit, and are life."

There is a chain of mind action connecting cause and effect in all the activities of life. This chain is forged by man, and its links are thoughts, words. Jesus laid great stress upon the power of the word. Yet He was wise in the injunction that His words should be kept; that is, men were to keep before them the ideal that He had. This realm of the ideal is the realm from which the word draws its substance, and its character determines the result.

The "sayings" of Jesus were charged with tremendous significance. They raised the idea of man and God far above what had ever before been conceived. They so far transcended the thought plane of the people that even His followers could not accept them, and many "walked no more with him." It is but a few years since the followers of Jesus began to grasp the power of the word as taught by Him. Who in the past has taken Jesus literally and sought to overcome death by keeping His sayings? Many have believed in His doctrine, and a great ecclesiastical industry has been built upon it as a foundation; but who has taken in full faith the *words* of Jesus and made them flesh of his flesh and bone of his bone by not only believing in them but by saturating his mind with them until they reincarnated themselves in his body? This achievement is the secret of every spiritual demonstration; it is not only a concept of what is true of Being but a carrying out in thought, word, and act of that concept.

If I can conceive a truth, it follows that there is a way by which I can make it manifest. If I can conceive of omnipresent life as existing in the omni-

present ethers, there is a way by which I can make
that life appear in my body. When once the mind
has accepted this as an axiomatic truth, it has ar-
rived at the point where the question of procedure
arises. No one ever fully sees the steps he is to take in
reaching a goal. He may see in a general way that
he is to go on from one point to another, but the
details are not definitely clear to him unless he has
gone over the ground before. The architect tells the
builder to follow the plans. So in this demonstration
of the spiritual powers that are ready to find expression through man he must be willing to follow the
directions of one who has proved his efficiency by
demonstration.

We all intuitively know that there is something
wrong in a world where poverty, suffering, and sor-
row prevail. We would not, any of us, create such a
world. We all want to see these things blotted out
in this world. This is the index pointing the way to
the possibility of doing so. Whatever we see as
wrong is for us to right. Lack of health is not prevalent in God's universe, and if such lack appears any-
where it is the work of man, and it is our duty to
do away with it.

There is a way, the "highway of the Lord." Will
you take that way? It is a broad way, and there is
room for everybody. Jesus called it the kingdom of
the heavens and said that "all these things" should
be added to those who sought it. This implies that
you do not have fully to enter this kingdom in order
to have the things added, but you do have to "seek."

You must turn your attention in the right direction; then they begin to come to you.

This is being proved by many thousands in this age who have accepted the promises of Scripture literally and are looking to God for every need, health included. They may not in the beginning of the seeking have a single thing to encourage them. They just accept the promise, proceed to carry it out in faith, and act as if it were true, and all at once new life and new strength are theirs. This encourages them to go on still further in seeking this kingdom of God, and eventually they will demonstrate the perfection of Christ.

These are they who have wisely used their one talent. They may not have caught sight of the holy of holies in the inner sanctuary, but they are gradually getting closer and closer to it. This is the step that everybody is commanded to take. Trust God in all things, and see the result made apparent by the mental currents that you set going all about you. You may not be able to point out just how each separate word of allegiance to the Father took effect, but as the months go by you will gradually observe the various changes that are taking place in your mind, body, and affairs. You will find that your ideas have broadened immensely to begin with. The little world has been transformed into a big world. You have begun to think about realities instead of appearances. Your mind is more alert, and you can discern when before you were in doubt. Your body is vital, and you are free from inharmony and weak-

ness. You are not so fearful. The consciousness that
there is a divine hand guiding the universe and you
has given you a feeling of security. This has extended to your body and your affairs. There is an
absence of prejudice and faultfinding in you. You
do not judge so harshly. You are more generous, and
others respond by being more generous too. Things
are coming your way now where you once thought
they were blocked.

This is not only true of your own particular life
and affairs, but if you are observing you will notice
its effect in a measure upon those with whom you
come in contact. They are getting more substantially
healthy and happy. They may not in the remotest
way connect it with you or your thoughts, but that
does not affect the truth about it. All things have
their cause, and every cause is mental. Whoever
comes in daily contact with a high order of thinking
cannot help but take on some of it. His mind takes
it on unconsciously just as his lungs breathe the air
of the room. Ideas are catching, and no man can live
where true ideas of wholeness and abundance and
peace are being held without becoming more or less
infected with them. "For none of us liveth to himself." Health is the divine heritage of every human
being.

CHAPTER IX

Healing through Praise and Thanksgiving

→»»→»×←←←-

I PRAISE *and give thanks that the strength and power of Thy Spirit now restores me to harmony and health.*

"Always praise the cooking of the cook" is the instruction of the veteran hobo to the novice. Experience has taught the gentlemen of the road that praise and thanks melt the hardest heart and often open the door to amazing hospitality. Tradespeople have found that "Thank you" has commercial value.

Metaphysicians have discovered that words which express thanks, gratitude, and praise release mind energy of mind and Soul; and their use is usually followed by effects so pronounced that they are quickly identified with the words that provoke them.

Let your words of praise and thanksgiving be to Spirit, and the increase will be even greater than when they are addressed to man. The resources of Spirit are beyond our highest flight of imagination. You can praise a weak body into strength, a fearful heart into peace and trust, shattered nerves into poise and power.

I give thanks for the Christ life now apparent in my mind and body.

It is an easy matter to give thanks for what we

have already received, but it is not so easy to give thanks for what we hope to receive. However giving thanks in advance brings to pass a present expectation. Remember what Jesus said about one's mental attitude in demonstrating spirituality: "All things, whatsoever ye shall ask in prayer, believing, ye shall receive." This may be rephrased in this wise: Pray believing that you have received, and you shall receive.

Christians who have discovered the hidden laws of the mind make it a practice to give thanks for health, for peace of mind, for all things that they desire, believing that God has given in Spirit that which is to appear in the visible.

I daily praise and thank the Spirit of life and health for constantly restoring me to perfection of body.

Praising and giving thanks liberate the finer essence of soul and body when we center our attention upon Spirit. Spirit is the dynamic force that releases the pent-up energies within man. The energies have been imprisoned in the cells, and when released are again restored to action in the body by the chemistry of creative Mind. The perfection of this restoration is in proportion to the understanding and industry of the individual.

Every thought we loose in our mind carries with it a certain substance, life, and intelligence. So we might call our thoughts our "thought people." Whenever praise is bestowed on these thought people, who are intelligent, it is carried to every part of the body and through the ether to a large area of our soul aura, and our whole consciousness and everything about us is tinctured with praise. Thus we prove what Jesus proclaimed, that when we seek His kingdom and His righteousness all things are added to us.

The prophets of old knew the power of increase inherent in thanksgiving. "Praise ye Jehovah" is repeated again and again in the Psalms, because the Psalmist knew that praise and thanksgiving divinely directed tap the mighty reservoirs of infinite Mind.

Jehovah-shalom gives me peace of mind, and I am harmonized and healed.

The Bible contains more high mysticism than all other books. But it requires study of certain fundamental spiritual principles to discern it. Spiritual things are spiritually discerned. Unless you call on your own innate spiritual light you cannot appreciate spiritual insight of those who wrote the books of the Bible.

The idea that all the Bible writers were equally inspired is fallacious. They were from every walk of life, and their inspirations were modified by their own mental bias as well as their surroundings. Moreover some of the most important revelations of fundamental principles are undoubtedly the result of borrowing. Although Moses was a trained mystic and inspirational writer, he did not originate all the allegories found in the books that bear his name. It is obvious from the testimony of religious records antedating the Hebrew Scriptures by thousands of years that Moses complied and edited for the benefit of the Israelites.

This discovery does not detract from the truth or importance of the writings but greatly enhances them. The very fact that these sacred writings have been preserved for untold ages points to them as possessing unusual value and as conservers of worth-while knowledge.

Studying the Bible in the light of the discoveries of modern science, we are amazed at the scientific accuracy of the statements in the early chapters of Genesis. Have men in past ages been wiser than those of the present or were they inspired beyond their understanding? For example, in the 3d verse of the 1st chapter of Genesis, God created the light on the first day, yet the sun, the supposed source of light, was not created until the fourth day. This supposed error in the orderly creative process often has been cited as evidence of crudity by Bible critics. But the very modern scientific discovery that the sun is not the source of light, that the sun merely radiates the light that originates in universal etheric waves proves that Moses was right. So what we call light is not the real light, but a luminous effect produced in our earthly atmosphere. So also all life originates in the ether, and not in the earth, where scientists have vainly sought it. When science admits, as it eventually will, that the ether is moved by omnipresent Mind, we shall have in the Bible a complete spiritual cosmogony.

The Bible is a perpetual revelation to Truth seek-

ers on account of its allegorical character. This is
especially outstanding in Genesis, which veils in
names and ordinary incidents some of the great
truths of creation. The names of the Divinity are
not all the same in the Hebrew. Elohim God represents the original Mind in creative action. *El* means
the strong and ever-sustaining one, and *alah,* to
swear or formulate by the power of the word. Here
also is implied plurality of attributes in addition to
masculine and feminine qualities. *Elohim* thus represents the universal principle of Being designing all
of creation. In the 2d chapter another name for
God is used—Jehovah God—metaphysically representing the executive power Elohim. This name is
also rich in occult significance. *Yahweh* is the original form, and its meaning is "the self-existent one"
at work or becoming known or revealing Himself to
His creation and through His creation. Yahweh revealed Himself to Moses as "I AM THAT I AM."
He reveals Himself to every one of us according to
our needs when we call upon Him. He revealed Himself to Jesus as the Father within.

The Hebrew teachers gave compound names to
Jehovah to meet every situation. That is, they invoked His I AM presence as a creative factor in producing the thing needed. When they needed supply,
they invoked Jehovah-jireh, "Jehovah will provide."
Jehovah-rapha is "the Lord that healeth thee." Jehovah-shalom is "Jehovah is peace" or "the Lord
send peace." The whole world needs peace today as
never before, and peace will not be ushered in until

men call on the name of Jehovah.

It may sound foolish in the sight of men for a small group of people to call on Jehovah-shalom to make peace in the midst of war, but great miracles have resulted from such action. Jehovah-shalom will save us from personal worry and fear of future ills. It was the Jehovah-shalom in Jesus that proclaimed, "My peace I give unto you: not as the world giveth, give I unto you. Let not your heart be troubled, neither let it be fearful."

I am a tower of strength and stability in the realization that God is my health."

It is the conclusion of the followers of Jesus that a new and original interpretation of His teaching has sprung up in the last half century. The adherents of this new religion, for such it seems to be, claim that they have a revelation of Christianity that far transcends the old in spiritual understanding and power. The new religion makes Jesus a demonstrator of scientific mind laws that any industrious student can understand and apply as Jesus applied them. In addition to this the new Christianity elevates man to a realm in which seeming miracles of healing become possible to those who train their mind to think spiritually, carrying out the admonition of Paul "Be ye transformed by the renewing of your mind."

As all the physical science books have to be rewritten since the discovery that electricity is the mother of matter, so all books of religion that ignore psychology will have to be rewritten.

The new Christianity claims that Jesus Christ understood the real character of space and ether as taught by science and that it is the home of a great and mighty life and intelligence that brought man and the universe into manifestation.

Instead of fighting modern science the new Christianity welcomes its discoveries as proofs of the veritable existence of the kingdom of the heavens that Jesus taught so persistently.

Instead of a heaven after death the new Christianity teaches a kingdom of the heavens existing now as a righteous state of mind. It teaches that man makes his heaven here and now by the formative power of his thought.

It is by way of this emphatic and constant emphasis on the formative power of thought that the new Christianity launches out into the deep. Instead of God's creating man with a mighty word fiat and arbitrarily following it up with vengeance and punishments, God is discerned to be a mind principle that requires the co-operation of its creations, because they are formed of it and in it and are so like it that there is virtual action and reaction between Creator and creation. This places the responsibility for conditions on both God and man. When we think and work in unity with the Father the results are universally good. When we work without reference to the inspiring Mind within our work is usually unsatisfactory. "My Father worketh even until now, and I work," said Jesus.

Then the carping critic cries, "Your religion is

psychology instead of Christianity." Our answer is that the new Christianity includes an understanding of psychology but does not stop with an analysis of the mind. It goes on to the highest phase of mind's possibilities, unity with Spirit.

When it dawns upon man that he has within him the primal spiritual spark of God, the living Word or Logos, and that through the Word he is identified with the original Mind, he has the key to infinite soul unfoldment.

Even though a person does not at first have this higher revelation of his sonship and unity with creative Mind, the assumption helps him to bring it to realization. Jesus developed in faith and power as He used His word. According to the text, He did not know that He could do absent healing by the power of His word before the centurion suggested it.

Never dampen your faith or the faith of another in you. Jesus exalted faith to first place in His healing work. "Be of good cheer; thy faith hath made thee whole." "When they cast *thee* down, thou shalt say, *There is* lifting up," said Eliphaz to Job. If there is appearance of sickness or weakness, affirm with all your faith the healing thought.

Through the Spirit of truth I now partake of Christ substance and Christ life in holy communion, and I am made whole.

At the Last Supper Jesus taught that the bread and wine that He consecrated were His body and His blood, and He told His followers to partake of them in remembrance of Him. He did not say that these elements were symbols of His blood and body but that they were essentially the same substance and life as His body. This also has been the teaching of the church, as interpreted by the Council of Trent: "Under each species and under each particle of each species Christ is contained whole and entire." This is the doctrine of transubstantiation, that the consecration by the minister of bread and wine changes the material elements to Christ elements, without affecting their appearance.

This doctrine has been attacked both within and without the church, the majority of ministers and laymen accepting it on faith as in some way related to the miraculous. But the discoveries of the elemental character of matter by modern science are revealing the universal unity of substance and the possibility of its transformation from one thing to another by changing the number and arrangement of the electrons in the atom.

According to modern science this whole universe of forms can be dissolved into energy, from which it may again be formed. Science does not say that the directive and formative power is man, but the Bible so teaches and especially Jesus. Jesus said that all power was given unto Him in heaven and in earth. He manifested His power in a small way by multiplying a few loaves and fishes to feed more than five thousand persons. In various other instances He demonstrated that He had an understanding of the transmutation of substance. He raised His flesh body to an energy level far higher in potential life and substance than any reached before.

As a race we have for ages been deprived in our consciousness of union with our creative source, and the result has been a gradual decrease in vitality until the body has lost the ability to hold its atoms together and consequently has disintegrated. Thus death has come to be accepted as in some mysterious way a part of the divine plan. Here again certain biological experiments with cells prove them to be possessed of an ability to reproduce themselves, which at least hints at physical immortality.

There are in the world today men and women who have followed the teaching of Jesus and have developed in their bodies a superenergy or life that not only permeates the physical structure but envelops it in a luminous aura that can be and is felt by both themselves and others. Spirit reveals that spiritual thinking breaks open the physical cells and atoms and releases their imprisoned life, which originally came from Divine Mind. Jesus carried this process so far that His whole body was transformed and became a conscious part of the Father life and intelligence.

In this way the substance and life of Jesus' body became a connecting link between our bodies and the body of God. Jesus merged His consciousness with the race consciousness and made Himself subject to our shortcomings in order to lift us up to spiritual life. This is the secret of His great sacrifice and sin offering.

When we understand that man has the power to

release the divine life imprisoned in the cells of his body and project it as spiritual energy, we have the key that unlocks many mysteries of personal influence. The vast difference between mediocre and great speakers and singers is not in voice and words but in invisible soul energies. We feel the presence before a word is uttered. For example, a music critic says of Toscanini, the great orchestra leader: "He brings a charge of electricity into the hall that cannot and does not enter in at any other time. If only certain persons felt this galvanization of the atmosphere one might be accused of romanticism or hero worship for mentioning it. But everybody feels it."

Thousands of great and near-great religious leaders have developed this "soul body," for that is what it is, but none has reached the high development of Jesus, who made it possible for us all to take advantage of His achievement and through Him attain eternal life.

All things and all conditions of body and affairs have their origin in mind, and it is in our minds that we make contact with the Christ Mind. The mind of Jesus Christ penetrates and permeates our race consciousness like the etheric waves from a mighty broadcasting station, and we can tune in at any time by simply concentrating mentally on the Christ life and Christ substance.

God and man, heaven and earth, and all the healing powers that be now unite in healing me.

Socrates, the wise man of Athens, once prayed that "Jove and all the gods that be" hear his prayer.

His idea was to invoke all the higher forces, counting them all worth while. All great men recognize the breadth, height, and depth of Being, that it is not comprehended in one name, but may be expressed in many. Paul preaching to the Athenians on Mars' Hill did not disdain their many shrines, said to be two thousand in number, but complimented them on their piety, at the same time proclaiming that he came as the representative of the "UN-KNOWN GOD" to whom they had erected an altar.

So we recognize that there is but one source of Being but that He is expressed in His Son Christ and manifest in His personal representative, Holy Spirit. The ancient Israelites had several outstanding names for Jehovah, each representing some special agency, as supplier, peace giver, guide, and the like. Some sects in our day pray to saints to execute the will of God in their behalf.

These all point to the fact that God is made manifest in a universe of executive powers, upon whom man can call as principle or as some form of personal agency.

This healing statement is recommended particularly to those who have depended upon temporal remedies or persons for their healing. It will amplify and energize the healing idea to the point of omnipotence, because it recognizes all the healing potencies that faith has made substantial in the past and brings them all to a focal center in wholeness.

It is universally recognized that the whole human family has broken loose from the usual stabilized thoughts, that we are afloat in an atmosphere of doubt, that we are walking question marks asking one another at every turn: What next? What will be the outcome?

The world of materiality is ending. Science says that what we thought was a material atom was really the shadow of an amazing aggregation of protons and electrons pulsating with potential life, energy, and power. We have been perpetuating the world of materiality by our material thoughts. Now our dominant thinkers are letting go, and they are telling us that matter is merely the smoke screen of a universe of energy. As an eminent scientist says, "We live in a universe of waves, and nothing but waves."

Christian metaphysicians see the truth that our minds have been jarred loose from their material concepts and that they have not yet laid hold of the true concepts. We are mentally afloat in the cosmic ether, waiting for someone to show us how to lay hold of real, stable ideas. When men's minds lose their stability, chaos reigns in their affairs. Emerson said that when a man of ideas is born into the world kings totter on their thrones.

Jesus said that He came to fulfill the Law and the Prophets; that is, to demonstrate that natural and spiritual law are one. He foresaw this very period when the "powers of the heavens shall be shaken" —that is, the mental realms be broken up—and He attributed this phenomenon to the coming of the Christ as "lightning."

The 24th chapter of Matthew describes in symbols what is taking place in this century. Christ Mind is quickening the cosmic light, which science is interpreting as natural law. Those who see spiritually announce that the next great revelation will be that of the "prophets," those who discern spiritually that the cosmic ether and the Christ Mind are one and that the character and the manner of the coming of the Christ—as a mighty, all-infolding, spiritually quickening mind—is referred to in the very modern metaphor of lightning: "For as the lightning cometh forth from the east, and is seen even unto the west; so shall be the coming of the Son of man."

Jesus answers the flood of queries as to what we shall do when we are caught in a whirlpool of thought: "Seek ye first his kingdom, and his righteousness; and all these things shall be added unto you."

The present panceas for the ills of the world are all lacking in principle and will eventually be discarded, to be followed by the Christ plan, which will make all the products of the earth directly available to all the people of the earth. Before this Christ plan can be established governments must petition God for His intervention in their affairs; then the divine plan will be revealed.

I press forward with courage and boldness in the power of God, and I am healed.

In the 6th chapter of Revelation it is written: "And I saw when the Lamb opened one of the seven seals, and I heard one of the four living creatures saying as with a voice of thunder, Come. And I saw, and behold, a white horse, and he that sat thereon had a bow; and there was given unto him a crown: and he came forth conquering, and to conquer."

The "four living creatures" represent the four dominant factors in manifest life, which has its original source in the Lamb, which represents the pure, nonresistant life of Being.

The four horses and their riders are, first, "a white horse," representing the power of the Christ; secondly, "a red horse [war]: and to him that sat thereon it was given to take peace from the earth"; thirdly, "a black horse" (commercialism): "a measure of wheat for a shilling, and three measures of barely for a shilling"; and fourthly, "a pale horse: and he that sat upon him, his name was Death."

At no time in the history of the world has there ever been such activity in the riders of the three dark horses as right now. The prodigious preparations for war by nations, incited by the greed for gain will soon lead them to "let slip the dogs of war" unless the rider of the white horse comes forth "conquering, and to conquer."

Although all Truth students are praying for harmony in the settlement of earth's tribulations, they cannot help seeing the effect of thoughts of selfishness. The last section of this chapter in Revelation gives a symbolic description of the chaos to come among those who are not seeking to conquer under the banner of the rider of the white horse, Christ.

We hold that those who have had revealed to them the peace-giving power of the Christ mind should be unusually energetic in declaring it to be the dominant quality in the minds of men everywhere. Do not argue or contend with error but silently (and aloud if the occasion seems propitious) declare the presence and power of the Christ.

In the 7th chapter of Revelation is a symbolical description of four angels protecting the earth until the servants of God are sealed on their foreheads.

The forehead is the center of consciousness, which the understanding of Truth seals; that is, it secretly unites the consciousness with Christ. The number sealed is twelve thousand out of the twelve tribes. This is all symbolical and should not be taken literally. Man has twelve faculties, represented by the twelve tribes of Israel. When the consciousness in the forehead is illumined by Spirit, all twelve centers in the body automatically respond. "These are they that come out of the great tribulation, and they washed their robes, and made them white in the blood of the Lamb."

The "blood of the Lamb" represents the primal life of Being, which Jesus made accessible to all those who believe in Him as the revealer of the pure life of God the Father. This consciousness of spiritual life is mentioned in the 22d chapter: "And he showed me a river of water of life, bright as crystal, proceeding out of the throne of God and of the Lamb."

The concluding verses of the 7th chapter of Revelation reveal the joys of the faithful. Every member of Unity should study chapters 6 and 7.

It will require more than mortal fortitude and courage to cope successfully with the conditions that are imminent in human affairs, and we shall all need the help of a higher power. This higher power we shall find in the Christ Mind.

Cast out fear as far as the tribulations of the world are concerned. Affirm:

"I press forward with courage and boldness in the power of God, and I am healed."

CHAPTER X

"I Am the Way, and the Truth, and the Life"

→≫→≫≫≪←≪←

JEHOVAH GOD *restores me to health and wholeness.* Words are quickened by those who speak
them and they pick up and carry the ideas of
the speaker, weak or strong, ignorant or wise,
good or ill. Thus words descriptive of deity have
been personalized in the thought stuff of the race
and those who invoke them in prayer and meditation are given a spiritual impetus far beyond what
they would receive from common words. It is a fact
that the name Jehovah came to be held in such rever-
ence by the rabbis that they never spoke the word
aloud. Jesus said that His words were so charged
with spirit and life that they would endure longer
even than heaven and earth.

Next to Spirit the word of Spirit is the most
powerful thing in existence. The author of the Book
of Hebrews says "that the worlds have been framed
by the word of God." We read in Genesis that "God
said" and it came to pass. And God said, "Let us
make man in our own image, after our likeness."
Thus we see that man is the incarnate word of God,
and it logically follows that our words bring forth
whatever we put into them. Study the 1st chapter
of John. Jesus said that a man will be held accountable for his lightest word.

Spiritually classified, the Jehovah of the Old Testament is identical with the Christ in the New. One who heals by the power of the word should become familiar with the inner meaning of all words and use those that appeal to him as possessing the greatest healing potency. Jesus promised that He would unite with the Holy Spirit in helping those who called upon Him. Unity healers have found that this promise is fulfilled when they concentrate in prayer and positive affirmation on the presence of the Holy Spirit and Jesus Christ. A new and strong contact is felt with spiritual life, as if it were a mighty battery, when the name *Jehovah God* or *Jehovah-rapha* ("the Lord that healeth thee") is spoken silently and audibly; then the ethers quicken with the name and shower spiritual life on both patient and healer. The word *Jehovah* or *Yahweh* is charged with spiritual power far above and beyond any other word in human language.

I am raised to perfection in mind and body by the healing power of Jesus Christ.

Quite a few Truth students ask why we emphasize Jesus Christ so strongly in our writings and statements of Truth. Spiritual psychology proves that the name of a great character carries his mind potency and that wherever his name is repeated silently or audibly his attributes become manifest. Jesus knew this and commanded His disciples to go forth in His name. The marvelous works they did prove that they exercised power far beyond anything warranted by their education or previous ability, power springing directly from Spirit.

Every thinker who studies the life and teachings of Jesus readily admits that He attained an understanding of spiritual things far beyond that of any other man that ever lived. His mind touched heights far beyond those of other advanced searchers for Truth. As we unfold spiritually we see more and more that Jesus understood the finer shades of metaphysical reasoning and related His mind and body to both ideas and their manifestation.

Jesus demonstrated that He understood the healing power stored up in the body, which He said is released through faith. "Thy faith hath made thee whole." Jesus identified Himself and His name with the sacred name of the Hebrew dispensation, Jehovah, and added another link to that long chain of names and events that brought forth the perfect man ideated by God-Mind, Jesus Christ.

As a directive head is essential in any army, militant or spiritual, so in every forward movement of the human family there must be a leader. The leader is chosen because of his ability as a demonstrator of the principles adopted by the group he represents. The religious principles taught and demonstrated by Jesus were not originated by Him, nor did He claim them as a "discovery." He said that Moses wrote of Him, and He often quoted Moses, but with an interpretation quite different from that of the popular religious leaders. He told them that they studied the Scriptures expecting through them to attain eternal life when the only way to attain that life was through

Him, and they would not come to Him. Right here Jesus emphasized the spiritual man, the I AM in man, as the only way by which man can enter the kingdom of God.

Jesus was undoubtedly the greatest of all exponents of the impersonal I AM, which is revealed to man when he opens up the supermind within his own soul. Jesus Christ's real name is Jehovah, I AM. The personal man Jesus is merely the veil or mask worn by the spiritual man Christ or Jehovah. We are all, in our personality, wearing the mask that conceals the real, the spiritual, I AM. Jesus shattered that mask and revealed the spiritual man. He also taught the way by which we may all do what He did and thus fulfill the destiny implanted in us by the parent Mind.

There are many distractions to keep us from finding the one door into the inner kingdom and many voices calling to us that they will show us the easy way, but Jesus Christ is the only one that appeals to those who are grounded in principle.

Any declaration man may make in which the name *Jesus Christ* is used reverently will contact the spiritual ether in which the Christ I AM lives and will open the mind and body to the inflow of spiritual healing rays. These healing rays are very much superior to the ultraviolet rays that come from the sun or our best medical appliances, because they minister to the mind as well as the body.

Thy vitalizing energy floods my whole being, and I am healed.

The most inclusive name for Being is Jehovah God. Jehovah represents the individual I AM and God (Elohim) the universal Principle. When man thinks or says "I am" he is potentially giving freedom to the seed ideas that contains in its spiritual capacity all of Being. The natural man in his narrowed mental comprehension barely touches the seed ideas that expand in the Christ man to infinite power. The more we dwell upon and expand our I AM the greater looms its originating capacity before us. When Jesus proclaimed, "Before Abraham was born, I am," He realized that the I AM preceded all manifestation, however great, and was capable of infinite expression.

The proposition that the seemingly insignificant individual I AM contains infinite creative capacity appears absurd to the thoughtless, but we have numerous examples of extraordinary capacity for expansion in the little seeds that bring forth gigantic trees. The Scriptures plainly teach that men may become gods. Adam was expelled from the Garden of Eden because Jehovah realized that he might appropriate eternal life and live forever in his ignorance.

When man realizes that "death and life are in the power of the tongue" and begins to use his "I am" statements wisely, he has the key that unlocks the secret chambers of existence in heaven and earth.

The Christ substance (body) and the Christ life (blood) are accessible at all times and in all places to the one who awakens his soul to spiritual omnipresence. The table of the Lord is spread everywhere for those who believe on Him as Spirit and in their Spirit affirmation eat of His body and blood. The appropriation by His followers of His life and substance is the very foundation of salvation through Jesus Christ. The mere acceptance intellectually of the teaching that we are saved by the blood of the Lord Jesus and the partaking of the bread and wine in a perfunctory manner will save neither mind nor body. The only thing that will do it is the understanding that Jesus raised His body life and substance out of the race consciousness into Spirit consciousness and that with our minds poised in that consciousness we can lay hold of the Spirit elements that will save us to the uttermost.

Nearly everyone needs both mind and body healing, and those who give faithful attention to the law as it operates in man are rewarded by demonstrations of healing. Jesus healed "all manner of disease," the same Jesus has broadcast that healing Spirit to the uttermost ends of the earth, and today all who will may be made whole.

The Christ life quickens and heals me.

Although millions have testified that they have felt the quickening life of Christ, other millions doubt if such a thing as the Christ life exists.

The unseen forces have always been an enigma to the masses, and even those who are expecting the unseen to spring forth suddenly into some marvelous manifestation do not recognize it when it comes to pass. It is said that when Marconi demonstrated to a group of scientists in Paris the power of radio waves,

they doubted his claims and sought in various ways
to discover the concealed wires, which they were
sure were being used. So every unseen force man uses
has had to prove its existence by some visible manifestation that can be mechanically demonstrated. But
are there unseen forces that cannot be mechanically
demonstrated? The answer is that all unseen forces
can be mechanically demonstrated and that they are
being demonstrated every day the world over, but
scientists have not yet recognized as mechanical all
the devices through which man brings unseen forces
into manifestation; for example, his own brain and
the radio. These with many other unseen forces come
under the head of mechanism.

Brain cells are the only material things that will
transmit mind, and man has never yet been able to
invent so fine a piece of mechanism outside his own
organism. But brains are mechanical, and man does
build and use them in expressing his intelligence.

The fact is that each of us builds a brain especially designed and fitted for our individual use and
for no one else's. All attempts to turn our brains over
to others in hypnosis or mediumship will prove abor-
tive in the end.

In radio terms your brain cells correspond to the
tubes in a combined broadcasting and receiving set,
and you have tuned them to certain wave lengths
and turned on the power. If you have not been in-
formed of your innate ability to turn on or off the
mind waves, you are functioning in the established
race programs of personality: what your ancestors

have thought, what other people think, and what little thought you can conjure up yourself. Unless your mind has been quickened by the light of spiritual understanding, you are living in a little three-dimensional world whose beginning and end is sin or a falling short of the divine ideal.

"If a man keep my word, he shall never see death."

"I am the resurrection, and the life."

Jesus stressed the power of words, especially His words. In the parable of the sower He said, "When anyone heareth the word of the kingdom." Here He referred to the Logos, the creative Word, which framed the worlds, according to John. The creative Word or Logos is also identified as Holy Spirit, which is carrying forward the ideas of God as they unfold in the manifest universe.

As the Word of God, the Logos, is creating in the universe (body of God) so man's word is creating in his universe (man's body). That is why Jesus said that we should be judged by our words. We are creating a little universe in which the cells of the body correspond to the planets of the solar system. "And I say unto you, that every idle word that men shall speak, they shall give account thereof in the day of judgment."

The "day of judgment" to us is any day that we get the fruit in body and affairs of some thought or word that we have expressed.

The creative power of man's word is in proportion to his understanding of God-Mind and his unity with its law. The creative power of most men does not get beyond their own body consciousnesss, because they know very little about Spirit and their relation to its laws. The better we realize our spiritual relationship to creative Mind and conform our thoughts and words to its laws the greater is the power of our words. Jesus "tuned in" to Divine Mind until that Mind reinforced His mind and raised it to superhuman capacity. It was in one of His moments of mental exaltation that He declared, "The words that I have spoken unto you are spirit, and are life."

We have thought that we were to be saved by Jesus' making personal petitions and sacrifices for us, but now we see that we are to be saved by using the creative principles that He developed in Himself, and that He is ever ready to co-operate with us in developing in ourselves by observing the law as He observed it. "I in them, and thou in me, that they may be perfected into one."

Thus we see that when Jesus said, "If a man keep my word, he shall never see death," He meant that we should realize the life-giving properties of the creative words of God as He had realized them, that we should have no consciousness of death.

I have new life in Christ and I am healed.

To attain this realization of the word of life we must create currents of life in our bodies as Jesus did in His. Of all man's possessions the most valuable is life. "For what shall a man be profited, if he shall gain the whole world, and forfeit his life? or what shall a man give in exchange for his life?"

When Jesus uttered these words He was explaining to His disciples that He was about to pass through a transformation in which He would give up His physical life, though He would continue His manifestation in a spiritual life. They did not understand Him, and Peter "began to rebuke him." Jesus told them they did not understand the things of God "but the things of men." Up to this day the passing over of the natural life into the spiritual life is not fully understood by Christians. It is almost universally interpreted as something that takes place after the death of the body, while in fact it is a transformation of the issues of life while the body is intact. Paul said, "I die daily." So Jesus could not have appeared after His crucifixion in the same body if He had not daily given up the physical life and daily put on the Christ life. It is a step-by-step or cell-by-cell transformation.

What did Jesus mean when He said, "If a man keep my word, he shall never see death"? Did He mean death of the soul? There is nothing in His teaching to warrant such a conclusion. He meant that we shall escape physical death if we identify ourselves with the creative Word in Him, the Logos.

Then to understand the new life in Christ we must give attention to that mystical Word or Logos, because in it are wrapped the principles that, planted in our minds, will spring into new life in mind and body.

Eternal life and strength are here, and I am made whole through Jesus Christ.

Among the seven sacred names given to Jehovah by the Hebrew priesthood is "Jehovah-shammah," meaning "Jehovah is there." Jehovah is the name of the ever-living I AM. When the mystic desired to commune with the omnipresent life he did not speak the name aloud but silently intoned, "Jehovah-shammah!" This pervasion of his I AM with the ever-living I AM harmonized the spiritual man with his source, and the individual was merged with the universal.

A certain mystery has always accompanied the use of the sacred name, and the priesthood gained their ascendancy over the people by performing marvelous works through the silent and audible intoning of words charged with thoughts of spiritual power.

However a priest must undergo discipline to acquire mastery of the elemental forces that function in mind and body. A cursory reading of Exodus conveys the idea that for forty years Moses was a shepherd, tending the flocks of his father-in-law Jethro, priest of Midian. But his mastery of nature, as evidenced by his works in Egypt, plainly shows that he understood the control of matter by mind better than did the magicians of Egypt, although he was versed in their magic.

The followers of Jesus did marvelous works in His name, but that name was also used by those who were not His immediate disciples, and they succeeded in casting out demons so well that John complained about it. Jesus said, "Forbid *him* not: for he that is not against you is for you." So we find that a person's name identifies him with his character. If that character is mighty in spirituality and power, he who invokes it in his prayers is automatically raised into a like sphere of power and what he says comes to pass. "And whatsoever ye shall ask in my name, that will I do, that the Father may be glorified in the Son."

Salvation through Jesus Christ is not accomplished by looking forward to freedom but by realizing that we are now free through His freeing power, which we are using to cut the bonds with which our thoughts have bound us. Then we have only to establish ourselves in real life and strength by understanding that these attributes of Being are omnipresent and that our affirmations of that presence, will cause us to become conscious that we do now and here live, move, and have our being in eternal life and strength.

In the name and by the power and authority of Jesus Christ I am made every whit whole.

Man gives a name—that is, "character"—to every idea that comes into consciousness, and whatever he conceives a thing to be, that it becomes to him. So it is written in Genesis: "Whatsoever the man called every living creature, that was the name thereof."

Jesus taught and demonstrated that man is master of a kingdom far beyond the consciousness of the natural man, but accessible to those who open their mind to its laws and observe those laws in thought and act.

The official declarations of a representative of a country are recognized by all as worthy of credence.

Jesus represented the kingdom of the heavens, and we, His agents, take possession of that kingdom in His name and declare that we are vested with authority to bring spiritual forces to bear that will restore man to his primal perfection.

In the 3d chapter of Acts is recorded the healing by Peter of a man lame from his birth; and Peter says, "In the name of Jesus Christ of Nazareth, walk. . . . and immediately his feet and ankle-bones received strength. And leaping up, he stood, and began to walk; and he entered with them into the temple, walking, and leaping, and praising God."

When the people were greatly astonished at this marvelous healing and gathered around Peter and John, Peter explained, "Ye men of Israel, why marvel ye at this man? or why fasten ye your eyes on us, as though by our own power or godliness we had made him to walk? . . . And by faith in his name hath his name made this man strong."

Shakespeare says, "Good name in man and woman . . . is the immediate jewel of their souls." But even Shakespeare, with his psychological insight, never realized how good a name would be or to what heights of power it could lift one who applies the laws of Spirit in its use.

Those who have searched diligently to know God and His Son Jesus and have prayed for the light of Spirit find that they possess a certain confidence and faith in the very name Jesus Christ and that to the one who speaks it the name draws creative forces far beyond mental comprehension.

Hence we should have confidence in the promises of Jesus that those who in faith use His name shall do the marvelous wonders that He did and even greater works of a spiritual character.

Read in the 16th chapter of Mark what are the signs of a real follower of Christ and see if you are measuring up to them: "And these signs shall accompany them that believe: in my name shall they cast out demons; they shall speak with new tongues; they shall take up serpents, and if they drink any deadly thing, it shall in no wise hurt them; they shall lay hands on the sick, and they shall recover."

By the grace of God through Christ Jesus I am made whole.

Jesus knew what He had accomplished in breaking the mortal mesmerism of the race, and He boldly proclaimed His ability to help all those who join Him in seeking to effect a direct union with creative Mind.

As Jesus healed in Galilee so He is healing in the same spiritual realm of radiant health today. "To him that overcometh, to him will I give to eat of the tree of life, which is in the Paradise of God." "I am the way, and the truth, and the life."

CHAPTER XI

Healing Power of Joy

-->>>->>X<<-<<<-

I REJOICE *and am glad because Thy harmonizing love makes me every whit whole.* All healing systems recognize joy as a beneficent factor in the restoration of health to the sick. "The joy of Jehovah is your strength." This statement is based on a principle recognized by all who help to bring about strength of mind and health of body. An old country doctor used to tell how he healed a woman of a large cyst by telling her a funny story: at which she laughed so heartily that the fluid broke loose and passed away.

The mind puts kinks in the nerves in ways beyond description. A thought of fear will stop the even flow of life in some nerve center deep down in the body, forming a nucleus where other fears may accumulate and finally congest the blood concerned in some important function. The impact of energy of some kind is necessary to break the dam. Physical exercise will sometimes do it, or massage, or electricity; but these are temporary remedies. None of them has touched the cause, which is mental: fear.

There are various methods of erasing fear from the mind and preventing its congestions in the body. One of the most direct and effective shatterers of fear is laughter. Laugh your fears away. See how ridiculous they are when traced to their source.

Nearly all persons have some pet fear, and they give up to it without trying to find its source.

The nerves surrounding the heart are most sensitive to thoughts of fear, and when mind and body are strenuously excited the fearfully charged nerve cells grab the heart and hold it like a vise. Businessmen who live in a world of sharp competition and constant risk of loss with few exceptions are subject to this kind of fear.

Christian metaphysicians of course know that the only permanent cure for the ailment is a heartfelt trust in God as the one and only source of good to man. A daily prayer for wisdom and divine guidance in the conduct of one's affairs will restore peace and harmony to mind and body, and health must of necessity follow.

I will sing unto the Lord a new song of harmony and health.

That there is an intimate relation between happiness and health goes without question. When you feel good you sing either audibly or silently. Singing promotes health because it increases the circulation, and a good circulation is a sign and promoter of health. If the blood stream were never congested and all the nerves and pores were open and free and were swiftly carrying forward their appointed work, there would never be an abnormal or false growth in the body. It follows logically then that we should cultivate those mind activities which stimulate naturally the currents of life in the body. One of these, and a very important one, is joy.

No one likes to take medicine even when sugar-coated, because there is an instinctive feeling that it will do no good. Besides it usually tastes bad. But nearly anyone can sing a little song, and those who have tried it right in the face of suffering will tell you that it is a marvelous health restorer.

The reason that singing restores harmony to tense nerves is that its vibrations stir them to action, thus making it possible for the ever-waiting healing Spirit to get in. The organ of the human voice is located right between the thyroid glands, the accelerators of certain important body functions. To a greater or less degree every word you speak vibrates the cells up and down the body, from front brain to abdomen.

The Spirit of health, or as the doctors call it, the restorative power of nature, is always right at hand awaiting an opportunity to enter in to make whole and to harmonize all discords in the body. Back of every true song is a thought of joy. It is the thought that counts in the end, because it is the thought that invites the healing Spirit. Consequently we should sing with the thought that the Lord is right with us and that His joy is giving our words the healing unction; as Jesus said, "that my joy may be in you, and *that* your joy may be made full."

When men think a great deal about spiritual things and especially about God as an indwelling spiritual presence, both mind and body are thrilled with joy, a feeling of satisfaction, and a tendency to break out in songs of gladness. This is not confined to Christians; persons everywhere, in every age, have told of an inner glory and happiness when they got into the habit of concentrating their mind on God. The great philosopher Spinoza wrote so much about God that he was known as the "God-intoxicated man."

Pythagoras taught that the universe is God's symphony and that all the suns and planets sing as they swing their way through the heavens. All nature has a language and a song for those who listen. Shakespeare says:

"And this our life, exempt from public haunt,
 Finds tongues in trees, books in the running brooks,
 Sermons in stones, and good in everything."

Shakespeare often quoted from the Bible, and he may have got his idea that trees have tongues from I Chronicles 16:33: "Then shall the trees of the wood sing for joy before Jehovah."

> *"My mind is cleansed by Christ;*
> *My life flows swift and strong;*
> *The peace of God wells up within,*
> *My soul bursts forth in song."*

Some people think it almost a sacrilege to sing when they feel bad. They think that that is the time to groan, and they usually do. That is the way the mortal looks at it, and that is the way you may happen to feel, but you can quickly be released from the prison of pain or grief if you will sing and praise and pray.

First sing in your soul—you can sing 'way down inside of yourself—then you will soon be singing with your voice. So we lay down the metaphysical law that everybody should know how to sing. Everybody can sing. It does not make any difference what your previous thoughts have been about your ability to sing, it does not make any difference what you think about it at present, and it does not make any difference whether you can sing or not; cultivate the singing soul and you will some day break forth into a singing voice.

This is a creative law, and it is a law that everyone should know and use, because through the vibrations of the voice joined with high thinking every cell in the body is set into action, and not only in the body but out into the environing thought atmosphere the vibrations go and break up all crystallized conditions.

The whole universe is in vibration, and that vibration is under law. Chaos would result if the law were not supreme. Each particular thing has its rate of vibration. Heat, light, and color are different rates of vibration in one field of primal energy. Different colors are caused by the different frequencies of the vibrations as they strike the eye. But what causes vibration? We answer Mind.

The cells of the body are centers of force in a field of universal energy. There are no solids. That which appears solid is in reality the scene of constant activity. The eye is not keyed to the pulsations of this universal energy and is therefore deceived into believing that things are solid. All energy and life are governed by laws of spiritual harmony. If the mind that receives sound vibrations is in spiritual consciousness, the body responds to the higher activity. If our mind were trained to think thoughts that harmonized with Divine Mind, we could hear the music of the spheres.

You can drive away the gloom of disappointment by resolutely singing a sunshine song. I believe that we could cultivate the power of music in connection with the understanding of Truth and thus rend all the bonds of sin, sickness, and death. The world needs a new hymnal, with words of Truth only and music so strong and powerful that it will penetrate to the very center of the soul.

Our body is now tuned to the divine harmony; we shall find the keynote by listening in the silence to the singing soul.

The new life in Christ fills me with zeal to live, and I am healed.

In putting on Christ—that is, developing the supermind—every faculty has to be raised to supermind proportions. The exact mathematical degree of power necessary to "synchronize" oneself with the "kingdom of the heavens" in which the supermind functions has not been revealed to human consciousness, if indeed it can be. An eminent British astronomer says that he has discovered that God is a great mathematician, and the logical conclusion of all wise philosophers is that everything in the universe both seen and unseen is under mathematical law. "The very hairs of your head are all numbered," said Jesus.

Jesus also said that He came to bring more life

to slow-moving humanity. More vital force now is and always has been the crying need of people everywhere. Disease germs run riot in anemic persons. The cause of such conditions is mental: there is a lack of vital interest in life and a disinclination to assume its responsibilities.

Ralph Waldo Emerson once said that no great work was ever accomplished without enthusiasm. Enthusiasm is another word for zeal, and zeal is a great stimulator of man. You cannot think of or repeat the word zeal without evoking a certain mental thrill that spurs you to action in some direction if you repeat it over and over. This brings us back to the point we mentioned about everything having a mathematical infusion; that is, everything is impregnated with mathematics. Every word we speak goes forth from our mouth charged with atomic energies that vibrate at a definite numerical rate. According to science every atom is composed of protons and electrons, the number of electronic elements in an atom determining the character of the substance. Now we see that modern science is proving the truth of Jesus' statement that we shall be held accountable for every word we speak. Our minds determine the character of our words and what the mind determines the mouth obediently utters, its words loaded with constructive or destructive electrons all mathematically arranged to build up or blow up both ourselves and our aims and ideals. We are perfectly aware that some persons are overzealous, that they consume their vitality by talking and acting without wisdom: "The zeal of thy house hath eaten me up." Such persons are so enthusiastic in externals that they lose contact with the source of things, the inner mind, and they destroy the body, the temple of the living God. However these are the minority. The great majority lack zeal in doing even the most ordinary things, and even the overzealous would find a much-coveted and needed poise by linking their minds with the Christ.

The beginning of the culture of the mind that enables it to make contact with the realm of creative ideas is faith, and faith is superenthusiasm. You must have such confidence in your ability to make union with creative Mind that you fuse the two and the invisible elements melt and fall into the mold you have made for them.

When we know that every word is mathematically linked with certain creative ideas and that Divine Mind has made it possible for every one of us to draw upon these ideas mentally, we have the key to all creative processes. "Whosoever . . . shall not doubt in his heart, but shall believe that what he saith cometh to pass; he shall have it." Here in a nutshell Jesus has stated the law and its fulfillment. The one and only reason that we do not always succeed in our demonstrations is that we do not persist in our mental work. If we have never tested our faith in God and His mathematical laws, we must begin to discipline our minds and raise our thoughts to the point where they abandon the slow inertia of the natural man for the speed and spring of the spiritual man. This is accomplished by prayer, meditation, and the repetition of true words. It is not the vain repetition of words over and over, parrotlike, but the quiet realization that there is a listening Mind and a ready host of great ideas at all times waiting for us.

I am at peace because I trust divine justice to regulate my mind, body, and affairs.

The mind may be compared to the sea, which is calm or stormy according to the wind that moves it. Thought utilizes the substance of the mind and forms that which man ideates.

A restful state of mind is greatly to be desired because of its constructive character. When the mind is lashed by a brain storm the cells of the whole organism are shattered and exhaustion ensues. Nervous prostration is the result of exhausted nerve force.

Man's whole character is determined by the thoughts for which he allows a place in his mind. A strong man or a weak man is what he is because of repeated thoughts of strength or weakness. Steadfast affirmations of peace will harmonize the whole body structure and open the way to attainment of healthy conditions in mind and body. The reason that prayers and treatments for health are not more successful is that the mind has not been put in a receptive state by affirmations of peace.

The Mind of Spirit is harmonious and peaceful, and it must have a like manner of expression in man's consciousness. When a body of water is choppy with fitful currents of air it cannot reflect objects clearly. Neither can man reflect the steady strong glow of Omnipotence when his mind is disturbed by anxious thoughts, fearful thoughts, or angry thoughts.

Be at peace and your unity with God-Mind will bring you health and happiness.

We all should practice delightful, happy, joyous states of mind. It is such thoughts that open the way for the ever-present Father-Mind to pour out its splendid resources into our mind and through us into all our affairs.

Thou art my life unfailing, and I rejoice in Thy abundant, buoyant health.

No one can understand the real character of God without a metaphysical study and analysis of mind and its properties. To think of God as an enormously enlarged man, as most persons do, entangles one in a maze of wrong conclusions concerning the nature and creative processes of Being.

Think of Being as an aggregation of ideas with potential creative capacity but governed in its creative processes by unalterable laws. Mentally see those ideas projected into action in a universe evolving a self-conscious creature possessed of free will called man. As man develops through the combination of those original ideas, behold him arriving at a place in his evolution where he realizes his power of self-determination and consciously begins to choose as his own field of action the many pleasant activities of the universe and to combine them in his own way.

This phase of man's development is symbolized

in the Edenic allegory as Adam and Eve eating of the fruit of the tree of the knowledge of good and evil. The tree that bears the fruit of pleasure in the midst of man's body garden is the sympathetic nervous system. Satan, sensation, tempts Adam and Eve —man—to appropriate or eat of this tree without listening to the voice of wisdom, Jehovah God. The result is unbridled and unlawful development of the sympathetic nervous system with excess of pleasure (good) followed by a corresponding reaction of pain (evil).

Jesus regained this lost Eden and showed us how to regain it by likewise identifying our minds with God-Mind. His prayer was "Not my will, but thine, be done."

Christ is the name of the God-Mind imaged in everyone. When we identify ourselves with that image, we rise superior to the Adamic man and become unified with the spiritual man. It is in the strength of this supermind that we can say to the man of flesh, "I will; be thou made clean." This is the decree of the Christ in you to your conscious mind and its visible body; it is the exercise of the authority given to every child of God. "Decree a thing, and it shall be established unto thee."

And manifest substance flows from a realm of light, according to the most modern conclusions of physical science. James says, "Every good gift and every perfect gift is from above, coming down from the Father of lights." God ideas are the source of all that appears. Accept this mighty and all-productive truth and consciously connect your mind with the Father-Mind, and you will realize abundant health and true joy.

The Holy Spirit life heals me, and I radiate health to everybody and everything.

Some persons think that when they quit lying they are demonstrating Truth. To quit lying is commendable but falls short of fulfilling the complete reformation of the Spirit of truth. In chapter after chapter of the Gospel of John, Jesus repeats the promise that He will send a Comforter, whom He names "the Spirit of truth," to those who believe on Him. In the 15th chapter we read, "But when the Comforter is come, whom I will send unto you from the Father, *even* the Spirit of truth, which proceedeth from the Father, he shall bear witness of me." In the 16th chapter we find these words: "I have yet many things to say unto you, but ye cannot bear them now. Howbeit when he, the Spirit of truth, is come, he shall guide you into all the truth." "And I will pray the Father, and he shall give you another Comforter, that he may be with you for ever, *even* the Spirit of truth . . . for he abideth with you, and shall be in you."

The Spirit of truth is the mind of God in its executive capacity: it carries out the divine plan of the originating Spirit. It proceeds from the Father and bears witness of the Son. We have in the operation of our own minds an illustration of how Divine Mind works. When an idea is fully formulated in our minds and we decide to carry it out, our thoughts change their character from contemplative to executive. We no longer plan but proceed to execute what we have already planned. So God-Mind sends forth its Spirit to carry out in man the divine idea imaged in the Son.

It is very comforting to know that Spirit is cooperating with us in our efforts to manifest God's law. God in His divine perfection has seemed so far removed from our human frailties that we have lost heart. But now we see that Jesus taught that God is intimately associated with us in all our life's problems and that we need only ask in His name in order to have all needs fulfilled.

The Spirit of truth is God's thought projecting into our minds ideas that will build a spiritual consciousness like that of Jesus. The Spirit of truth watches every detail of our lives, and when we ask and by affirmation proclaim its presence, it brings new life into our bodies.

Again the Spirit of truth opens our minds to God's law of supply and support, to the existence of a universal etheric thought substance prepared for man's body sustenance by infinite Mind. We have thought that in answer to our prayers God in some mysterious manner brought about the marvelous demonstrations that we had. Now we see that there has been prepared from the beginning an interpenetrating substance that, like a tenuous bread of heaven, showers us with its abundance.

But we must not only ask but bring the Spirit into our consciousness by affirming its abundance to be the source of all our good. Then perfection will begin to be manifested right in the face of apparent negation. Remember the invitation of the Master "Hitherto have ye asked nothing in my name: ask, and ye shall receive, that your joy may be made full."

CHAPTER XII

Holy Spirit Fulfills the Law

→>>→>><<<-<<<-

THE SPIRIT *of wholeness quickens and heals me.* The Spirit of wholeness is called the Holy Spirit in the New Testament. In classical mythology it is called Hygeia. Modern medical men refer to it as the restorative power of nature. It has been recognized by savage and civilized in every land and age. It has many names, and they all identify it as a universal urge toward perfection in man and the universe and toward keeping things going regardless of any interfering force.

We may look on this restorative power as merely the tendency of the cells in an organism to retain their homogeneity, and when we look at it in this light our consciousness robs it of any of the divine qualities it may possess. This is the way the scientific world regards what we call the Holy Spirit. To such a view the Holy Spirit has no warm heart. To persons holding such a view the Holy Spirit is not the Comforter referred to by Jesus but merely an abstract principle that works just the same way whether it is praised or blamed.

But to the Christian metaphysician the Holy Spirit is just what the name implies, the whole Spirit of God in action. In the Hebrew Jehovah is written *Yahweh, Yah* being masculine and *weh* feminine.

In the New Testament Christ stands for Jehovah. Jesus talked a great deal about the Holy Spirit: that it would bear witness of Him, come with Him, and help Him to the end of the age.

Do not be misled by the personality of the Holy Spirit and the reference to it as "he." This was the bias of the Oriental mind, making God and all forms of the Deity masculine.

Holy Spirit is the love of Jehovah taking care of the human family, and love is always feminine. Love is the great harmonizer and healer, and whoever calls upon God as Holy Spirit for healing is calling upon the divine love.

Just here, in connection with the Holy Spirit is an important point for a good Christian healer to consider. Do not regard the Holy Spirit altogether as a restorative principle without feeling, sympathy, or love. This reduces your healing method to intellectual logic and the slow process of mental science. Under this method the patient must always be educated in Truth principles before he can be healed. No instantaneous healing ever takes place under this method.

The Holy Spirit is sympathetic, comforting, loving, forgiving, and instantly healing.

> "Who forgiveth all thine iniquities;
> Who healeth all thy diseases."

Do not fear to call mightily upon the Holy Spirit, who has all compassion and healing power at His command.

*Thy perfect plan of bodily perfection is now
made manifest in me.*

That Mind, which designed the universe, must
have planned for man, its leading citizen, a body in
harmony with the universe is good logic. This conclusion does not require inspiration but merely common sense.

The religions of every race have taught this perfection of the body but have usually assumed that
it was to be given to God's elect in some heavenly
place after death. They have not thought it possible
that the body of flesh with its many apparent defects
could be transformed into an ideal body. In con-
sequence man has put the stamp of inferiority upon
his body, and through the creative power of thought
he has built into the race mind a consciousness of
corruptible flesh instead of the inherent incorruptible
substance of God-Mind.

This race thought of man's body as impure and
perishable in time became so dense that no human
thought could penetrate it. It was gradually consum-
ing the little life left in human bodies and would
have ended with their total destruction if it had not
been for Jesus, who was incarnated as demonstrator of the perfection and immortality of man's
body.

That the body of flesh had within it life elements
that could be released and incorporated into a much
finer body has always been beyond the comprehension of the sense mind, and it required a physical
demonstration to convince men that it could be done.

Jesus made that demonstration, and some of His followers were convinced that the body with which He appeared to them after the Crucifixion was the identical body that suffered on the cross. Thomas, for example, was allowed critically to examine that body for the marks and wounds of the cross, and he found them and was convinced.

But the majority still doubted and do so to this day. Not understanding that the body that Jesus occupied for the thirty-three years of His earthly incarnation could be transformed into an imperishable body, they have assumed that Jesus really died on the cross and went to heaven where God gave Him a glorious body. There is no foundation for this in the facts given in the New Testament.

"God is Spirit," said Jesus. "Know ye not that your body is a temple of the Holy Spirit which is in you, which ye have from God?" wrote Paul. Here are two statements by accepted authorities on fundamental Christian principles. If God is Spirit and He dwells in man's body, that body must have within it certain spiritual principles. Here modern science comes to the rescue of primitive Christianity, telling us that the atoms that compose the cells of our body have within them electrical units that, released, can change the whole character of the organism. Jesus had attained an understanding of the law that releases these electrical units, and He knew before the Crucifixion that He could thus make His body unkillable; which He did.

When Elohim God created man in His likeness,

He imprinted upon man's supermind two body pictures: first the picture of a natural body, and secondly
the picture of a spiritual body. In the primal cell He
then inclosed the elements necessary to the building
of the natural and the spiritual body; that is, electricity on the inside and flesh on the outside. Then
to man was given dominion and authority over these
living atoms and cells out of which he must build
mind and body into visibility. As God created man,
His image and likeness, by the power of His word so
man, God's image and likeness, projects his body
by the same power.

Our physical bodies are carried in our minds as
thought and they obediently reflect every mental attitude. When in the course of our evolution we discern that an allwise Creator must have designed perfection for all His creation and we begin to affirm
that perfection, then the transformation from the
natural to the spiritual body begins, and it continues
until our body is wholly regenerated and appears ob-
jectively in its divine perfection.

*Thou art the strength of my life, and I am made
whole.*

The mighty truth that everything in this universe
is the product of thought few persons let sink deeply
into their minds. Mankind have wandered in thought
so far from the parent Mind that they do not reflect
or observe that everything they do originates in
mind. A very little observation and reflection will
convince anyone that mind acts on matter in every part of life. The story of creation begins in the

first chapter of the Bible with God's command that the dry land appear. Then in the second chapter Jehovah God formed man out of the dust of the ground. Not only here in the beginning do we find mind molding matter; all through the Bible runs the same story. Jesus said of His body that He could raise it up.

When the truth dawns on man that mind rules matter in both the great and the small, he has the explanation of myriad mysteries, strange episodes, reputed miracles. This great truth that mind is the source and moving factor in all creation would, if studied and practiced, prove of tremendous worth to religion, science, and art. Jesus taught the supremacy of mind in many illustrations, but His followers have not understood the metaphysical significance because they have not analyzed the mind or directly applied its spiritual powers. When Jesus said that the Father was within Him and that the words He spoke were not His but the Father's, He must have referred to God as an interpenetrating mind.

Everything in this universe has both its mental and its physical side. Heaven and earth are parallel everywhere. Even the so-called elemental forces of nature are dual. Our men of science are puzzled because light sometimes appears as waves in space and again as particles. To a metaphysician the waves express the mind and the particles the matter. When Jesus walked on the water He blended His mind with the mind of the water and it obeyed His concentrated will.

Nature's mind is always the servant of man's mind when man lifts his thoughts to Spirit. Nature will even obey a determined will on an inferior plane of consciousness. Concentration of will as practiced by metaphysicians of the Orient, African witch doctors, and a horde of occult adepts bears testimony to the power of the mind to manipulate matter visible and invisible.

> *"I sow no seeds of care and strife;*
> *But those of love, and joy, and life."*

It is reported that a great philosopher, Herbert Spencer, once said substantially that he would gladly turn his life over to any creative force that would plan and carry it forward without his having to take any responsibility.

Because of the many blunders that the natural man makes in his life, such a shifting of responsibility would be popular on the part of many who have ideals that they are unable to fulfill because they are bound by material limitations. Also in the secret recesses of all of us there lurks the conviction that there is a power somewhere that may be invoked to show us a hidden way into the city of success. We think we should willingly follow any path in life if we were sure that we were being led by the hand of supreme wisdom.

In his famous soliloquy Hamlet heaps up the measure of the burdens of life with the subtle argument that they could be shifted by death:

For who would bear the whips and scorns of time,

The oppressor's wrong, the proud man's contumely,
The pangs of despised love, the law's delay,
The insolence of office and the spurns
That patient merit of the unworthy takes,
When he himself might his quietus make
With a bare bodkin? who would fardels bear,
To grunt and sweat under a weary life,
But that the dread of something after death,
The undiscovered country from whose bourn
No traveler returns, puzzles the will
And makes us rather bear those ills we have
Than fly to others that we know not of?

Spiritual insight reveals that Hamlet is right. We cannot escape life's experiences, be they ever so rough, by fleeing to another environment. All the conditions in this world have been constructed by the people who inhabit the world, and each individual is a builder of it and personally responsible for his immediate environment.

It is the mind that makes the man, and the mind and the thoughts of the mind endure even though the body be dissolved. So let no man think that he can escape the creations of his mind by breaking the physical chains that bind him to the earth. Nor does death in any of its phases relieve him of the states of mind that dominated him at the time of passing. The law of God is not mocked at any time or under any circumstances. "Whatsoever a man soweth, that shall he also reap." What we have sown in the flesh we shall reap in the flesh unless we repent, change our minds. When we do repent, we shall break mortal thoughts and ascend into a spiritual thought realm, the kingdom of God. This ascension we do not attain by dying physically but by dying to ill thoughts and living in true, good thoughts while still in the flesh. "Yet in my flesh shall I see God."

"The Word became flesh, and dwelt among us," says John in the very first chapter of his gospel.

Of all the great spiritual teachers of the ages Jesus has given us the most vivid and vital evidence of God as Father and guide. We say as Philip did, "Show us the Father, and it sufficeth us." The disciples were looking for a flesh-and-blood God. Do not the majority of Christians today look forward to seeing sometime, somewhere, a flesh-and-blood God sitting on a throne? Jesus replied, "He that hath seen me hath seen the Father."

He then explained that He was in the Father and the Father in Him. Yet His listeners did not understand, because they had not been trained to think metaphysically. God is Spirit, omnipresent Spiritmind; and in Him "we live, and move, and have our being."

"God lives in me; no more I pine;
For love, and health, and joy are mine."

That God is the animating principle of all creation is not a new or startling teaching. It has been the conclusion of thinking minds ever since the birth of logic, and it will never be discarded so long as the faculty of logic continues to be exercised. Where there is an effect there must be a cause, and no amount of sophistry will erase the straight line from premise to conclusion. Timid men will cry pantheism and scare both themselves and others with a bugaboo they do not understand. Nevertheless the fact remains that intelligence and design and all the other evidences of an omnipresent planning Mind are so palpable in us and the world about us that we cannot boast of our sanity and at the same time deny them.

When logic presents these mighty truths to us and we begin to turn our attention to the omnipresent principle eternally active and flashing its presence into us and the whole universe, we awaken within ourselves a consciousness of it, and it begins to think and plan through us. This is the first movement of Omnipresence, creating man as a self-conscious replica of itself, that is, of God. This replica is the Son of God or Christ, the exact reproduction in miniature of the mighty cosmic Mind. When this man of cosmic Mind arrives at full manifestation of Himself in habitation and place, we have Jesus Christ, the Son of God or God glorified in man. Jesus in ecstasy beholding this climax exclaimed "Glorify thou me with thine own self with the glory which I had with thee before the world was."

So if we have not begun our glorification by realizing this quickening life within, let us commence right now to recognize it in thought and word. James Russell Lowell wrote, "It may be that the longing to be so helps make the soul immortal." A great truth, spoken by a great man. Desire from within shoots a ray of energy from the imprisoned I AM to the all-infolding Spirit, and a thread of golden light unites

parent and child. Darwin taught that desire for light
in the protoplasmic cell shot a ray from its center
to its surface and formed the primary eye. If this be
true, and it seems logical, it is possible for us to
animate the thirty-nine trillion cells estimated by
Doctor Crile to be present in the body and eventually
make them all luminous, as did Jesus. Thus science
is revealing to us the movements of mind in forming the primary or physical body, which by the
quickening of the Spirit is raised to the glorified immortal body.

We should not lose sight of the fact that the
completion of this glorified body that God has
planned for us devolves on us. We must become
conscious of God-Mind and co-operate with it in
making His plan manifest in us. As Jesus said, "My
Father worketh even until now, and I work."

The childlike simplicity of this primary work
seems so insignificant that great men who have
delved into philosophy and worked with weighty intellectual problems deem it beneath them to become
as a little child and concentrate their thoughts on
nursery rhymes. They do not realize that instead of
molding and animating the cells of their bodies they
have projected their thoughts outwardly in speculat-
ing about the universe and its laws. So the cells left
to themselves gradually starve for want of mind
stimulation and finally die.

If you, dear reader, have attained eminence in
some earthly field of action and yet have not demonstrated health, it may be that you need to take sound

words in some simple form and go unto your Lord.

The Spirit of Him that raised up Jesus dwells in me, and I am made whole.

Paul wrote, "But if the Spirit of him that raised up Jesus from the dead dwelleth in you, he that raised up Christ Jesus from the dead shall give life also to your mortal bodies through his Spirit that dwelleth in you."

Few Christians realize the vital truth in this statement by Paul, although it is but one of many of like character to be found in his writings. Paul taught that what Spirit did for Jesus it would do for all who follow Him and adopt His methods of spiritual self-development.

Jesus claimed like results for His followers. In Matthew 19:28 it is written, "Verily I say unto you, that ye who have followed me, in the regeneration when the Son of man shall sit on the throne of his glory, ye also shall sit upon twelve thrones, judging the twelve tribes of Israel."

The promises of the power of Spirit to transform man from a mortal to an immortal state are producing a great company of spiritual-minded persons in the world today who work in the silence and speak but little about their heavenly experiences. In this way Spirit is forming a mighty Christian army that, when the need arises, will come out of its obscurity and save our civilization from extinction.

Although these spiritually quickened souls, often widely separated, may be working alone, they are bound together by the Holy Spirit, and the bond of brotherhood that unifies them is far more enduring than any human relationship. They are developing latent faculties of the soul that will make them superpowered men and women.

In order to establish and perpetuate the new order of life that is being poured into earth's mental atmosphere from on high it is absolutely essential that a people be prepared who can make use of the finer forces of the mind. The great initial outpouring of Spirit took place at the Pentecostal baptism more than nineteen centuries ago. The few who received this primal baptism are the seed from which has sprung a multitude. The trillions of cells forming the body of Jesus swim in omnipresence awaiting our appropriation. They are the living, quickening seeds of new life.

I am strengthened and healed by the power of the Spirit in the inner man.

We all need a better acquaintance with that phase of creative Mind that reveals and forms a connecting link between the Most High and the mind of the natural man. Most of us have not made conscious contact with the Spirit within but are thinking and acting in the outer crust of our being. Consequently we cannot hold communion with God in His omnipotence but must have a mediator or equalizer of the light and power that proceeds from the originating source of existence.

This is illustrated in high-powered electric systems: a transformer is necessary to lower the voltage and adapt it to the capacity of small industrial

motors. If the full current from one of the big electric cables were turned directly into our small motors
it would burn them up.

If the full current of God life were turned directly into the ordinary man's nervous system, it
would destroy it. An equalizer has been provided—
the Holy Spirit or Spirit of truth—through Jesus
Christ.

Our human family has lost contact with the Spirit
of truth, and our only salvation is through a soul
strong enough to re-establish the connection. Jesus
Christ released the electric atoms in His body and
formed a conduit in the ether through which divine
life is again flowing to the inhabitants of this planet.
Without this purified life substance we should be
unable to receive life or any message direct from
God.

In John 14:16 Jesus said, "And I will pray the
Father, and he shall give you another Comforter,
that he may be with you for ever, *even* the Spirit of
truth: whom the world cannot receive." Again in
John 16:14 He makes His identity with the Spirit of
truth stronger: "He shall glorify me: for he shall
take of mine, and shall declare *it* unto you."

All who have faith enough to believe these
things are comforted and guided by the Spirit of
truth. Read John 17:20: "Neither for these only do
I pray, but for them also that believe on me through
their word."

It is the Spirit of truth that talks to us in dreams,
visions, and inner urges. The more we acknowledge

the Spirit as our indwelling inspiration and life the stronger its consciousness will be to us.

Through the Spirit of truth God moves the whole creation; hence any man may constantly increase his understanding of the source and relation of all things by claiming his unity with the Spirit of truth.

QUESTION HELPS

BE THOU MADE WHOLE

CHAPTER I

1. In what respect do the words *Christ* and *Jesus* differ in meaning?

2. What is the supreme attainment of every man?

3. Is it possible for the Christ to experience death, burial, and resurrection?

4. When and where does resurrection take place? How did Jesus resurrect His body?

5. Do the words we use have any bearing on the results we get?

6. Why is it that man has not brought forth a greater degree of the Christ perfection?

7. Are infirmities permanent? How overcome?

8. Why did Jesus never give His personality any credit for the wonderful works He did?

9. Do all men have access to the Christ within?

10. Should man give more attention to the healing power of nature?

11. Should the student give his undivided attention to one system of development or should he study many? Explain fully.

12. Are there any short cuts into the kingdom of heaven?

13. Explain what is meant by the "end of the world," as brought out in the lesson?

14. Describe the means by which Jesus undertook to establish the kingdom of heaven on earth.

GOD PRESENCE

CHAPTER II

1. How may we know more of God and of ourselves?

2. Explain the meaning of "God is the health of His people."

3. Does God ever will man to be sick? Does He ever use His power to punish His creations?

4. How may we say that the attributes of God are expressed?

5. Should man ever think of God as being separate from him or outside him?

6. Explain how mind is the connecting link between God and man.

7. What is the proper procedure in realizing God as health? Is it looked on as practical by the world at large?

8. Explain the "still small voice."

9. Explain God as principle. Should the truth that God is principle lead us to infer that He is cold and unfeeling?

10. What part does man play in the forming of things?

11. Is God ever absent from His creations?

12. Since intelligence is the light of the world, how may we increase our intelligence?

REALIZATION PRECEDES MANIFESTATION

CHAPTER III

1. How are we able to know that mind is the source of all things?

2. How should we regard miracles?

3. Is it possible for us to do the works that Jesus did?

4. Is it possible to explain the laws governing religion from a scientific viewpoint?

5. What part does concentration play in our demonstrations?

6. Give the metaphysical meaning of the word *realization*.

7. What does faith have to do with the realization of one's ideals?

8. Are all prayers answered?

9. The text mentions a realm where no effort is required to gain the answer to questions. Explain.

10. What is the supreme realization of man?

PRODUCING RESULTS

CHAPTER IV

1. What states of mind are necessary if we are to realize perfect health?

2. To what phase of being should a person give his attention in order to understand the Scriptures?

3. How can healing be instantaneous?

4. Explain the meaning of the word *sin.*

5. What is it to forgive sin?

6. Should one ever think of oneself as being born in sin? What should be one's viewpoint?

7. What is the foundation of the Jesus Christ kingdom?

8. What part does love play in our unfoldment?

9. Explain fully the meaning of the Trinity.

10. What mental attitude should man have toward his body?

THE OMNIPOTENCE OF PRAYER

CHAPTER V

1. Why is it necessary to affirm a thing one already knows to be true?

2. Should everyone pray? Why?

3. Explain why Jesus advised us to ask for what we want.

4. Is asking always a part of prayer? What other forms of prayer are there?

5. Is it ever good for one to be self-righteous?

6. What is the key to all mysteries?

7. What part do faith and understanding play in a perfect demonstration?

8. What is the real foundation of effective prayer?

9. Is it essential to have great faith in order to demonstrate?

10. Is silent prayer more effective than audible prayer? Why?

11. What state of mind is necessary if we are to receive clear revelations?

12. Why are some healings slow even though prayers are said?

GOD SAID, AND IT WAS SO

CHAPTER VI

1. Explain fully in your own words the power of healing words.

2. Did Jesus ever write? Through what channel have we received His words?

3. From what standpoint did Jesus say that His words are spirit and are life?

4. Does the word of itself have power? What must we do to give full force to our words?

5. Is Truth ever the formulated doctrine of any church, creed, or sect? Where may we find Truth?

6. What must we do to keep successfully in mind the words of Jesus?

7. Is moral goodness always an indication of spirituality?

8. What determines the character and the results of our words?

9. Is it necessary for us to feel our oneness with God in order to believe in His omnipotence?

10. What does the healing of the man at the Pool of Bethesda represent?

11. Is it ever possible for anyone to do our spiritual work for us?

12. Explain how Jesus made His teachings available to all.

INDISPENSABLE ASSURANCE

CHAPTER VII

1. Is man's desire for a fuller and more excellent life a natural and orderly one? Explain fully.

2. Give in your own words a definition of faith. Is it

natural for man to have faith?

3. Is it a falsehood to deny sickness in the face of its appearance?

4. How are we to get more life?

5. Is it a fact that faith is blind?

6. How are we to emulate Jesus? Is it necessary to do so in order to do the works of God?

7. Give three steps that are necessary in demonstration.

8. Would you call Jesus a master scientist? What did He mean when He said, "In my Father's house are many mansions"?

9. Is it better to seek understanding through intellectual reasoning or through divine inspiration?

10. Just what do our thoughts and words have to do with our demonstrations?

11. Is it always necessary for us to be receptive in order to be healed? Does God ever do things for us against our will?

12. Give the difference between a genius and an ordinary man from the metaphysical viewpoint.

13. Is it sufficient to be inspired by an ideal, or is something else needed?

14. Should one ever take the attitude that things as they are cannot be changed?

15. Explain what is meant by giving up the personal and taking up the universal.

THE FULLNESS OF TIME

CHAPTER VIII

1. What part does order play in life?

2. Explain fully the power of words.

3. Is there any limit to the power of thought?

4. What should be our attitude toward hurry?

5. How may we become conscious of our I AM?

6. How is soul growth related to bodily health?

7. Explain the relation between law and order. What part does law and order play in the divine scheme of things?

8. What is the difference between natural law and divine law?

9. Were the works that Jesus performed really miracles? Why?

10. Is it good to deny the existence of the things of the world?

11. Is it necessary to enter fully into the kingdom in order to realize results?

12. Give some of the signs that follow the giving of attention to Spirit. ———

HEALING THROUGH PRAISE AND THANKSGIVING
CHAPTER IX

1. Has praise any commercial value? Any spiritual value? Explain.

2. How is the body restored to perfection?

3. How should the various writers of the Bible be judged?

4. Is it possible for us to be of service in establishing peace on earth?

5. In your own words tell how the new Christianity and physical science are working together.

6. Where is heaven, and how is it formed?

7. Explain what Jesus meant when He said that the bread and wine was His body and His blood.

8. Does man have the power to form and reform the universal energy?

9. Is there more than one God?

10. Explain in your own words the meaning of the four horses mentioned in the 6th chapter of Revelation. ———

"I AM THE WAY, AND THE TRUTH, AND THE LIFE"
CHAPTER X

1. Explain why the word of Spirit is next to Spirit in power.

2. Compare Jehovah and Christ. How should one go about choosing healing words?

3. Why do we find it advantageous to use the name Jesus Christ?

4. Did Jesus discover the principles He taught and demonstrated?

5. Give the difference between the real spiritual I AM and the personality. How did Jesus handle this proposition? Is it possible for us to do likewise?

6. What is the difference between Jehovah God and Elohim God?

7. Does the individual I AM contain infinite creative capacity?

8. Can the unseen forces be mechanically demonstrated? How?

9. What did Jesus mean when He said that we should be judged by our words? What is meant by the "day of judgment"?

10. Explain fully the change from the natural life to the spiritual life. What did Paul mean when he said, "I die daily?"

11. What must be our viewpoint if we are to be saved?

12. Should we expect healing today the same as in the time of Jesus' ministry on earth?

HEALING POWER OF JOY

CHAPTER XI

1. Explain how joy acts on fear.

2. Explain the relation between happiness and health.

3. Do you think that singing can be of benefit toward the realization of perfect health?

4. Explain how the whole universe is in vibration.

5. What part does zeal play in our unfoldment? Explain fully.

6. What is the cause of man's seeming lack of vital energy?

7. Explain the importance of faith. How is faith quickened?

8. Does man's thinking have much to do with his spiritual progress?

9. Why is it necessary first to study mind in order to understand the real character of God?

10. What should we do to bring the Spirit into our consciousness?

———

HOLY SPIRIT FULFILLS THE LAW

CHAPTER XII

1. Explain the Holy Spirit from the viewpoint of the Christian metaphysician and the physical scientist.

2. How should a good Christian healer regard the Holy Spirit?

3. Should we ever hesitate to call on the Holy Spirit?

4. Did God create man with a perfect body or perfect-body idea?

5. Did Jesus die on the cross? Explain how He was able to resurrect His body.

6. Is it to our benefit to know that mind rules matter? Explain.

7. Is it possible to escape life's experiences by a change of environment or by death?

8. Can "ascension" be gained through physical death?

9. What did Jesus mean when He said, "He that hath seen me hath seen the Father"?

10. Is it necessary for man to become as a little child? Explain fully.

11. Why is it that man must have a mediator in order to contact God? Who is this mediator?

12. Since man has seemingly lost contact with Spirit, what is his only salvation?

INDEX

INDEX

About the Author

Charles Fillmore was an innovative thinker, a pioneer in metaphysical thought at a time when most religious thought in America was entirely orthodox. He was a lifelong advocate of the open, inquiring mind, and he took pride in keeping abreast of the latest scientific and educational discoveries and theories. Many years ago he wrote, "What you think today may not be the measure for your thought tomorrow"; and it seems likely that were he to compile this book today, he might use different metaphors, different scientific references, and so on.

Truth is changeless. Those who knew Charles Fillmore best believe that he would like to be able to rephrase some of his observations for today's readers, thus giving them the added effectiveness of contemporary thought. But the ideas themselves—the core of Charles Fillmore's writings—are as timeless now (and will be tomorrow) as when they were first published.

Charles Fillmore was born on an Indian reservation just outside the town of St. Cloud, Minnesota, on August 22, 1854. He made his transition on July 5, 1948, at Unity Village, Missouri, at the age of 93. To get a sense of history, when Charles was eleven, Abraham Lincoln was assassinated; when Charles died, Harry Truman was President.

With his wife Myrtle, Charles Fillmore founded the Unity movement and Silent Unity, the international prayer ministry that publishes *Daily Word*. Charles and Myrtle built the worldwide organization that continues their work today, Unity School of Christianity. Through Unity School's ministries of prayer, education, and publishing, millions of people around the world are finding the teachings of Truth discovered and practiced by Charles and Myrtle Fillmore.

Charles Fillmore was a spiritual pioneer whose impact has yet to be assessed. No lesser leaders than Dr. Norman Vincent Peale and Dr. Emmet Fox were profoundly influenced by him. Dr. Peale borrowed his catchphrase of *positive thinking* from Charles Fillmore. Emmet Fox was so affected by Fillmore's ideas that he changed his profession. From an engineer, he became the well-known writer and speaker.

Charles Fillmore—author, teacher, metaphysician, practical mystic, husband, father, spiritual leader, visionary—has left a legacy that continues to impact the lives of millions of people. By his fruits, he is continuously known.

Printed U.S.A.

55-3037-5M-10-96